CW00432215

Austr BUSH Cooking

Cathy Savage

photography by Craig Lewis

BOILING BILLY
PUBLICATIONS

www. boilingbilly.com.au

WOODSLANE

www.woodslane.com.au

A Boiling Billy Publication
under licence to Woodslane Press
An imprint of Woodslane Pty Ltd
10 Apollo St
Warriewood NSW 2102 Australia
Email: info@woodslane.com.au
Tel: 02 8445 2300 Fax: 02 9997 5850
www.woodslane.com.au

This third edition 2009, reprinted 2010, 2011, 2012, 2013, 2014
Copyright © text Cathy Savage and Craig Lewis 2009
Copyright © photographs Craig Lewis/Boiling Billy Images 2009

Design & layout: Vanessa Wilton (Billy Boy Design)

This publication is copyright. All rights reserved. No part of this
publication may be reproduced, stored in a retrieval system, or
transmitted by any form or by any means electronic, mechanical,
photocopying, recording or otherwise, without the express written
permission of the publisher.

If you have any suggestions for future editions of this book please write
or email us at:

Boiling Billy Publications
Nimmitabel, NSW
Ph: 02 6454 6162
e-mail: info@boilingbilly.com.au
web: www.boilingbilly.com.au

National Library of Australia Cataloguing-in-Publication entry

Author: Lewis, Craig (Craig William), 1966-
Title: Bush cooking : recipes for a gourmet outback experience /
             Craig Lewis, Cathy Savage.
Edition: 3rd ed.
ISBN: 9781921203930 (pbk.) - 9781921606489 (spiral)
Notes: Includes index.
Subjects: Outdoor cookery--Australia.
             Cookery, Australian.
             Cookery, Australian--Technique.
Other Authors/Contributors: Savage, Cathy
Dewey Number: 641.57820994

All Boiling Billy and Woodslane Press books are available for bulk
and custom purposes. Volume copies of this and our other titles are
available at wholesale prices, and custom-jacketed and even mini-
extracts are possible. Contact our Publishing Manager for further
information, on **+61 (0)2 8445 2300 or info@woodslane.com.au**

for safety's sake

Although the majority of the recipes in this book have been designed to be cooked on an open fire using a range of bush cooking utensils, there will be times throughout your travels in the bush when, it won't be possible to have a cooking fire.

Circumstances such as days of total fire ban or high fire danger, wet weather or campsites where open fires are not permitted will require the bush cook to plan meals that either do not require cooking or can be cooked on gas appliances.

Even on days of low fire danger it may be more prudent to use a gas/fuel stove for cooking instead of an open fire. Please use common sense in these circumstances as carelessness can lead to bushfires, causing destruction to forests and native animals as well as having the potential to threaten human lives and property. Fire restrictions are usually broadcast on local radio stations.

When constructing a cooking fire, use an existing fireplace if possible and make sure that all flammable material is cleared at least three metres from around the fire. It is also a good idea to keep some water handy in case of emergency.

Camp fires also have the potential to cause burns. Always use sturdy leather gloves when handling utensils on or near an open fire and if you are using camp ovens a camp oven lifter is essential. These are available from camping and outdoor stores or you can easily make your own from a steel rod.

Always carry a well-stocked first aid kit and know how to use it.

about the authors

After short stints in various occupations ranging from university student, office administration, sales and welfare, Craig Lewis and Cathy Savage decided that the wide open spaces of the outdoors was a much better workplace to spend their time than an office. Once the travel bug had bitten they began to knock out magazine and newspaper travel articles to help fund their habit and before long they stepped sideways into authoring books. In 1995 they saw a market for accurate and up-to-date guidebooks for people who, like themselves, love travelling and exploring Australia's great outdoors. Boiling Billy Publications was born.

Over the last 15 years the pair has travelled extensively throughout Australia. Along with the many adventures they have found on their doorstep, one of the highlights was an 18-month, 100,000 kilometre 4WD odyssey, visiting some of the very best outdoor destinations secreted away across this vast country.

As part of their extensive field research schedule, the pair generally camp out around 100 nights each year in an array of different campsites from the coast to the deserts. Many of the recipes for this book have been conceived, tested and refined during these camping adventures.

When not on the road travelling (that's the fun part) they throw down their swag on their secluded farm tucked away high up on the coastal escarpment in the Monaro region of New South Wales. The view from their office window looks out over the pristine Brogo Wilderness in Wadbilliga National Park.

contents

introduction

Does the term 'bush cooking' conjure up thoughts of some old-timer relaxing beside his campfire with a freshly caught rabbit braising in a camp oven? Bush cooking these days has well and truly changed from our early settlers cooking. As well as the changes to equipment and utensils, the food itself has changed.

Some people are under the impression that bush cooking only involves camp oven cooking ... not necessarily so. Yes, it's true that the camp oven's versatility makes it a great cooking utensil, however there's also the good ol' BBQ plate and grill, the ever faithful frying pan and saucepan, and now you can purchase portable smokers, folding ovens and portable spits.

As tastes have changed over time, cooking in the bush is no longer just damper made from water and flour accompanied by a rabbit or kangaroo stew. With Australia's wonderful multiculturalism and diverse eating tastes you can cook just about any of the meals you enjoy cooking at home and even some of those that you go out for.

Even the most patriotic Australian can tire of a BBQ every night, so you'll find recipes in this book using a number of different cooking methods. There is a good mix of BBQ and grilling, pan frying and camp oven cooking. You can even consolidate some meals using the camp oven instead of a frying pan, therefore saving space in your vehicle.

Camping trips are also the cook's holiday, so it's best to work on the 'keep it simple' system. All the recipes

included in Australian Bush Cooking are based on good eating as well as their ease to prepare and cook, and all have been successfully cooked in the bush. Some recipes will require a little more time to prepare and cook than others. Some will be best cooked when you have a standing camp for a day or so, others are nice and easy for when you are over-nighting while 'On the Wallaby'.

Menu planning is essential for all bush cooks. Nobody wants to miss out on their favourite meal! Some people might find meal planning a little too predictable. However, if you have a basic menu planned you can swap and change meals around so that when you get to camp you will at least know what to pull out of your tuckerbox. Don't forget to plan for your breakfasts, lunches and in between meals snacks!

When planning your menu remember to take into consideration where you will be travelling to, the time spent away from civilisation and shops, and if and when you will be travelling through fruit fly zones. You don't want to throw away any valuable fresh fruit and vegies.

The recipes in this cookbook use ingredients that are readily available Australia wide therefore creating no problems with restocking your supplies whilst travelling.

Along with the range of recipes you will also find inside this book some hints on packing before you go, the pros and cons of car fridges and eskies, details about cryovac meat, suggested items for your tuckerbox and suggested camp cooking equipment. You'll also find detailed information on the different types of cooking equipment available.

Remember, the secret to a happy bush cook is organisation and preparation. So on arrival at your camp it's well worth the time to first arrange for the

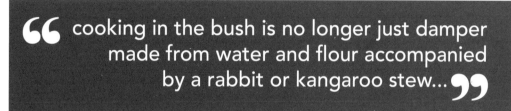

" cooking in the bush is no longer just damper made from water and flour accompanied by a rabbit or kangaroo stew... "

A good idea is to go for a wander down your local supermarket aisles to see what options are available for the bush cook. With food manufacturers so readily aware of everyone's need to save time when cooking there is a vast array of easy to prepare meals that can be utilised in the bush kitchen. As well, most of them are easy to pack and carry. A good stash of herbs and spices is paramount. Not only are they easy to carry but you can change the taste of a meal with a sprinkle of your favourite herbs or seasoning.

Don't forget when planning your meals to include recipes that can be prepared and cooked by the other half and/or the children. Believe us, there are times when the bush cook needs a rest from the fire.

cooking fire to be started, and then all other jobs can follow.

Happy bush cooking!

before you go

As the old saying goes: getting ready is half the fun. Here are a few ideas, along with a couple of tips on planning and preparing for your bush cooking adventures.

planning and packing

Planning and packing for any trip is largely an individual matter, with the amount of time spent on preparation and packing being dependent on the length of your holiday, the areas where you will be travelling to and the amount of space available for packing. Caravanners and long-term travellers, for example, will have different requirements to weekend campers.

Start by looking at your trip itinerary and then making a menu prior to leaving. This way you can work out what needs to be purchased before heading off and when and where you can restock your supplies. Also, when you have a menu planned it is a simple matter of collecting the ingredients for the night's dinner and packing them in an easy to reach position that morning, saving you time that night.

Along with the basic items that make up the bulk of the recipes in this book, there are now many items on the supermarket shelf that can be included in your tuckerbox and utilised along with your recipes. Items such as packet pasta, rice mixes and instant meals are useful additions to your pantry, as well as

bread mixes that come with their own yeast sachet. These are ideal to make up in the morning - you can leave them to rise during the day in a covered container whilst travelling and bake them at camp that night.

When packing ensure that you evenly distribute weight so all boxes are easy to lift and carry. We use sturdy plastic containers to store our food in - a wander around a hardware or large department store will reveal a range of containers that will suit your needs. You can also use heavy duty cardboard boxes for packing supplies, these are readily available and usually for free. Cardboard boxes with a lid that fits over the box, such as those used for apples and bananas seem to last the longest. One advantage of cardboard boxes over plastic is that they are easily disposed of when they are emptied, freeing up additional room in your vehicle.

Polystyrene foam boxes with fitted lids that are used to transport broccoli and similar vegetables can be used as coolers.

You will find things much easier if you have a number of boxes set aside for specific items. We have a smoko box which is kept in an easy to reach position so we don't have to unpack the vehicle when we stop for a break or for lunch. This box contains plates, bowls, cutlery, cups, basic cooking utensils, cutting board, tea, coffee, sugar and our favourite spreads such as honey, vegemite, peanut butter and mustard.

You might also consider separate boxes for cooking utensils, tinned food, fruit and vegies, packet foods and condiments. Your style and length of travel will dictate the number of food boxes you will require.

Where possible we usually purchase our sauces and condiments in plastic containers, otherwise we transfer the contents from the glass container to spare plastic containers. Plastic film canisters (ask at photo processing shop – yes, some people still use film cameras) are ideal for herbs and spices. We then place the labelled canisters inside an empty ice cream container or similar for easy packing.

If planning to travel on outback roads, which are often rough and corrugated, tinned foods will inevitably rub together, causing the labels to come off. In this situation it's a good idea to write the contents on the top of the can with a permanent marker pen. This saves the hassle of opening four tins of baked beans before you finally find the tin of peeled tomatoes you need for a recipe.

portable fridge or ice box cooler?

For the serious camper and traveller these are a great convenience. Portable fridges are either 'two-way' — those that run on both 12 volt DC, such as from your vehicle's battery, and 240 volt AC from a standard power point (some models require a power adapter); or 'three-way' which operate on the previous two power sources as well as bottled gas or LPG. Some two-way fridges may require an additional transformer to operate on 240 volt DC. The most popular type are the two-way units.

The drawback with portable fridges are their price, with quality units ranging in price from between $500 to $2000 or more, depending on size. In addition, if you are using your vehicle's battery as the fridge's sole power source it is wise to fit a second battery so you won't accidentally be left stranded with a flat battery.

If you only take a few camping holidays each year then hiring a portable fridge may prove to be more economical. Fridges can usually be hired for weekends, per week or longer.

Over the years we have used a number of different 12 volt fridges including the Australian made Autofridge and EvaKool as well as a Waeco, all of which have been both reliable and efficient during our travels.

The humble ice box cooler or 'Esky' has been keeping the beer cold on camping trips for years. Advantages of ice boxes are their cheap purchase price, compared to portable fridges, and their portability, as they don't have to be plugged into a power source they can be placed practically anywhere that is convenient. However, for ice boxes to be effective they need a supply of ice, which may or may not be readily available depending on your type of travel and style of camping. Block ice will keep longer than crushed ice. 'Dry ice' which is solid carbon dioxide, is an alternative to block and crushed ice, however, it is generally only available in cities and some larger centres.

cryovac® meat

A real boon for campers is Cryovac, a process of packing meat products in heavy duty plastic packaging and then removing all oxygen by a vacuum process (the removal of oxygen helps stop dehydration and degradation). Under specific temperature controls, the shelf life of meat can be extended to anything up to four or more weeks, depending on the type of meat. Cryovac or vacuum sealing not only prolongs the shelf life of your meat whilst travelling, it will stop any blood leaking into your fridge or esky from your meat packaging.

Time variations also occur depending on the type of meat. Beef will have the longest storage period – approximately 3 to 4 weeks when meat is kept at a constant 1° Celsius; lamb is next – around 2 to 3 weeks; then meat such as pork, chicken and processed meats, ie: sausages are best used within the first week.

Things to remember with cryovaced products:

- Meat with a bone can be cryovaced but must have bone guards in place.

- Do not use meat that has fresh additives – ie: herbs, spices, vegetables or fruit. If you are buying herbed or spicy sausages ensure that the butcher has used dried and sanitized ingredients.

- Dark cut meat should not be cryovaced. Use the freshest meat possible.

- It is an idea to always inspect meat packages each night to look for any wear or rub marks. If you find a package is punctured then use it for your next meal.

- Cryovac meat can be frozen then placed in your fridge or esky to defrost slowly. Freezing the meat will add some extra keeping time.

- When first opened, the cryovaced meat may have a slight confinement odour. This odour is just the mixture of the meat scent and carbon dioxide – rest assured that the meat is almost certainly fine to eat and the odour will dissipate after about five minutes.

When we travel we usually work out our menu in two week segments and have our local butcher cryovac enough meat to last us the two weeks, this includes bacon for breakfasts and meat for our evening meals including chicken breasts, mixed grills and other cuts of meat. We then generally don't need to shop until the end of our second week on the road. All we may need is either a small general store or service station to top up bread and milk. On longer jaunts we always try and leave a nice piece of cryovaced fillet steak tucked away in our car fridge for about 4 to 5 weeks. The aged steak is simply divine and melt-in-your-mouth tender when barbecued.

For further information about the cryovac process have a chat with your local butcher and discuss your camping and travelling requirements with them. They'll advise you on the best cuts to cryovac and their approximate keeping times.

cooking with gas

On all your trips to the bush it is a good idea to carry some type of liquid fuel stove to use when the weather prevents cooking over a fire or restrictions do not allow fires. For example, many national park and state forest camping areas in South Australia and some Murray River and Murrumbidgee River forests in New South Wales have solid fuel fire bans over the summer fire danger period, making a liquid fuel stove essential in these areas. Camping areas in other states also have solid fuel fire bans at times. Solid fuel fires include fires that are made from wood and/or heat bead products.

Please remember that on days of total fire ban the use of liquid fuel stoves, cookers and barbecues in open areas is also prohibited.

There is a vast array of stoves on the market using fuels such as unleaded petrol, butane gas and methylated spirits. However, the most common type of fuel stove burns liquid petroleum gas, or LPG, which is readily available in refillable bottles.

Single ring burners, that screw directly to the top of gas bottles, or the type which uses disposable butane cartridges are great for a quick cuppa or one pot meals. However the two and three burner free-standing stoves tend to be more practical if cooking for more than a couple of people. Although heavy, cast iron gas burner rings are another alternative.

Many of the recipes in this book can easily be cooked on a gas stove, even those involving camp ovens can be cooked by using a number of gas conversion attachments for camp ovens. These units, such as the Australian made Camp Oven Mate from Southern Metal Spinners or the Gas Conversion Kit by Hillbilly Camping Gear allow you to cook your favourite camp oven meals without the aid of coals from a fire. These are ideal in places that do not allow solid fuel fires.

carrying water

Water is one of the most important, but often rarely considered necessities for the bush cook. Good clean water is essential for both drinking and cooking.

It is getting steadily more difficult to rely on water from streams and rivers in the bush to provide safe,

uncontaminated drinking water so it is best to carry your own from a known, reliable source, or have the equipment or tables to sanitise water.

Carry water in containers that have been designed for that purpose and have not previously contained any other liquid that could contaminate or taint the water. It is safest to carry water in at least two

separate containers. If one splits or springs a leak you won't lose all your valuable water.

what rubbish!

It's a simple rule when it comes to rubbish — if you can carry it in, you can carry it out. It is okay to burn paper and cardboard packaging in your fire, but take everything else with you. We use plastic shopping bags for our rubbish which we then place in heavy duty garbage bags with draw top closures which are taken to the nearest rubbish disposal centre.

the tuckerbox

Your menu requirements and the length of your trip will determine what food you pack and take with you. Here are a few suggestions.

Tinned foods

- chinese vegetables
- tomatoes
- mushrooms
- tomato puree
- sliced beetroot
- corn kernels
- tuna
- sweet & sour sauce
- ham
- baked beans
- pineapple pieces
- spaghetti
- fruits
- 4 bean mix
- carrots
- soups
- peas
- capsicum
- smoked oysters

Packet foods

- dried beans
- long life milk
- french onion soup
- long life custard mix
- long life cream
- other soup mixes
- milk powder
- instant noodles
- custard powder
- biscuits, plain, sweet & crackers
- tomato paste sachets
- dried fruits
- cornflour
- self-raising flour
- marshmallows
- plain flour
- baking powder
- pasta
- instant pasta mixes
- instant rice mixes
- instant meal mixes
- rice
- cereals
- dried peas

Herbs & spices

- mixed herbs
- steak spice
- ground coriander
- chinese five spice
- curry powder
- chilli powder
- ground ginger
- cinnamon sugar
- garlic granules
- onion flakes
- mustard powder
- cajun spice
- cayenne pepper
- lemon pepper

Condiments

- oil
- tomato sauce
- bbq sauce
- worcestershire sauce
- satay sauce
- soy sauce
- salt & pepper
- stock cubes: beef, chicken & vegetable
- mustard
- chutney

fruit and vegetables

Before purchasing and packing fruit and vegetables, check your itinerary to see if you will be passing through fruit fly zones. it is best to leave purchasing these items until after you have travelled through the fruit fly exclusion zones otherwise they will need to be discarded at roadside disposal areas.

Fruit and vegetables will travel well outside a fridge or ice box, however it is best if you wrap each item individually in newspaper or butchers paper to protect them. also, by doing this, if one spoils it won't affect all of your supplies.

- potatoes
- zucchini
- onions
- broccoli
- pumpkin
- capsicum
- sweet potatoes
- cucumber
- carrots
- tomatoes
- cabbage
- apples
- oranges
- mandarins
- melons
- bananas

bush basics

types of equipment

From barbecues to billies and tripods to trivets, cooking in a bush kitchen is a whole lot easier with the right gear.

camp ovens

Camp ovens are one of the most useful yet, to many, most daunting pieces of bush cooking equipment. However, with a little practice the art of cooking in a camp oven will become rewarding as well as enjoyable. There are two types of camp ovens readily available, cast iron and spun steel.

Cast iron: these are the most common type of ovens available, with most cast iron camp ovens on the market these days being imported from overseas. The main advantage of cast iron camp ovens is their ability to hold an even heat for considerable periods, which is important when cooking on coals. Their main drawback is their weight. Also, there is a tendency for cast iron ovens to crack or shatter if dropped or stored incorrectly when travelling, even more so with the cheaper, thinner ovens that are generally not as heavy duty.

Spun steel: the traditional Bedourie style oven has a lid that can be turned upside down used as a frying pan. The other advantage of Bedourie ovens is that they are lightweight and compact, making them easy to pack. However, care is required with the amount of heat when using a Bedourie oven, especially when roasting and baking. Spun steel, being thinner than cast iron, transfers heat quickly and more intensely, which can result in burnt offerings if careful attention is not payed when cooking. The bedourie oven originated from the bedourie district in western Queensland and it is said that this type of camp oven became popular with drovers due to its light weight and robustness.

Spun steel camp ovens are also available in the traditional shape similar to cast iron ovens. These ovens are quite deep with a large dished lid to hold coals. Concentrating the heat on the lid helps avoid sticking and burning the food on the base of the camp oven.

barbecues and grills

Barbecues and grills/grates are available in a huge range of sizes and styles with most camping and outdoor stores having a large selection to choose from.

When selecting a portable barbecue you will find the types with folding or removable legs much more convenient to pack in your vehicle. Many portable barbecues have both a steel plate as well as a grate section which many people find more versatile than a barbecue that is all plate.

Circular steel plate barbecue: this style of barbecue is based on the old plough disk barbecue plate of rural Australia. One of the best we have come across (and is a permanent piece of our cooking gear) is the Biji Barbi which consists of a round steel plate with a slight dish to allow the fat and oil to run to the centre and drip through a small hole, adding fuel to your cooking fire. There are three folding legs as well as a folding handle.

Swinging grill: lightweight stainless steel grills are both simple to use and easy to carry. You can cook everything from steak to toast, and even boil the billy!

Swinging barbecue plate: this style of barbecue consists of a steel rod hammered into the ground with the barbecue plate swinging on a neck. A disadvantage with this type of setup, as with the swinging grill above, is that they are not suitable for very rocky or hard surfaces.

Folding grate and barbecue plate: a simple folding grate is a useful addition to your bush cooking gear: in fact, we consider one almost essential. This style of grate is available at outdoor and camping stores or if you are handy you might like to make one – a wire fridge shelf reinforced with a welded steel frame is all that's required. The folding legs are made from steel rod. A rectangular steel barbecue plate can be placed on top when required. Alternatively, your local engineering/welding shop could make one for you.

pots and pans

A frying pan and a couple of pots or saucepans are valuable additions to your bush cooking gear. These items allow greater scope for your bush culinary delights, especially for long term travellers and campers where a camp oven or barbie just won't do the job.

There is a range of different frying pans available on the market. Spun steel frying pans are light and easy to pack but due to their thin bases require careful management when cooking over a fire. On the other hand cast iron frying pans are heavy, but hold heat well over an open fire. Cast iron saucepans, like cast iron camp ovens, retain an even heat over an open fire but are heavy, and require careful packing and transporting.

smokers

Portable smoke ovens provide a tasty alternative to traditional cooking styles such as barbecuing and roasting. Just sprinkle a little sawdust in the bottom of the smoker, place your food on the rack, light the methylated spirit burner and you're smoking!

Circular stainless steel smoker: this large circular smoke oven manufactured by Togar Ovens has enough room to smoke anything from fish to chicken.

Galvanised smoker box: again, this can be used to smoke a variety of foods. Nipper Kipper Smoke Ovens come in galvanised iron or stainless steel, and

the manufacturers have developed an oven that folds for easy carrying.

billies and kettles

Billies and kettles are indispensable to the bush cook. In its simplest form a billy is a tin can with a wire handle usually used to boil water over an open fire for a cup of tea. There is much conjecture to the origin of the term 'billy'. One theory is that it came from the French word bouilli, which was a tinned French soup eaten by diggers on the early goldfields. The empty tin was then used to boil water for tea. Another explanation is that the word originated from the Scottish 'bally', which means milk pail.

Aluminium billy: lightweight, no-rust billy based on the original, no-frills design. Also available with a spout for easy pouring.

Tin billy: tin billies have a tendency to rust if not dried properly after use.

Enamel coffee pot style kettle: we find this type of kettle easy to use due to its spout and handle for easy pouring and close fitting lid.

Eco Billy: These are great for a quick lunchtime cuppa when you are on the move. Simply fill the billy with water, grab a handful of leaves, bark and twigs and set these alight. The billy is cyclindrical so the fire burns up through the centre of the billy. All you do is feed a few small twigs through the centre chimney and the water for your brew will be boiled in no time.

spits

Portable spits: portable spits make a great alternative to the camp oven roast. Spit motors generally run on 2 'D' batteries.

accessories

Having a few camp cooking accessories makes handling the camp ovens and other items easier and safer.

Camp oven lifters: the most convenient way of moving hot camp ovens around and lifting coal laden camp oven lids.

Oven trivet: placed in the base of the camp oven, this is used as a platform to put food on. Some camp oven manufacturers make trivets to suit their ovens or you can often find one to suit from a kitchenware shop.

Vegie ring: designed to sit in the top of the camp oven so vegies can be roasted whilst the meat is in the base of the camp oven.

Pot stand: designed to sit on the lid of the camp oven so cooking can be done in a frying pan or saucepan whilst roasting or baking, utilising the heat on the lid of the camp oven.

Jaffle iron: a cast-iron jaffle iron is an ideal item to have in your camp kitchen kit. They are perfect for cooking toasted sandwiches, either savoury or sweet. Just place the jaffle iron on top of some hot coals, turn it over regularly to ensure even cooking and you have a perfect toasted sandwich.

Shovel: essential for moving coals around your bush kitchen. You will require a shovel to place coals on the lids of camp ovens; move coals away from the main fire for simmering; dig a trench for a pit fire plus numerous other uses. If you have the room, such as a roof rack or trailer then a long handle shovel is the preferred type for bush kitchens, however any type of shovel will do the job. The great thing

about long handle shovels is that you can gather cooking coals for your camp oven without getting too close to the heat of the main fire.

Leather gloves: a pair, or preferably two, of sturdy leather gloves makes handling cooking equipment much safer and helps prevent burns and scalds.

care of cast iron & spun steel cookware

Cast iron and spun steel cookware, whether they be camp ovens, frying pans or saucepans, require special attention after use to prevent rust and corrosion forming (which will shorten the life of the utensil).

To clean your oven or pan warm it near the fire to loosen food particles, fat and oils then wipe out with paper towel or similar. This will leave a coating of oil on the inside of the oven or pan which will prevent it from rusting. For long term storage between trips thoroughly wash the oven or pan in hot soapy water and allow to dry, preferably near the fire or stove top. When completely dry wipe the inside of the utensil with cooking oil to prevent rust.

suggested equipment

Cooking equipment

- Matches
- Firelighters
- A two burner gas stove and gas bottle
- BBQ plate
- Grill or grate – excellent for placing frying pans, saucepans and camp ovens on over the fire
- 2 x saucepans with lids

- Frying pan
- Camp ovens – 2 if you have room
- Trivet – to use inside the camp oven to place dishes on
- 2 x billies
- Tripod hanger
- Spit (if spit roasting)
- Pie dish – to fit camp oven
- Loaf tin – to fit camp oven
- Pizza tray – to fit camp oven
- Camp oven lid lifters – to help lift camp ovens out of coals and also to take the lid off the camp oven
- Shovel - preferably long
- 2 pairs of thick leather gloves

Cooking utensils

- Mixing bowls – we use empty ice cream containers with lids. These can be used for serving and also for storage.
- Small measuring jug
- Tongs – short or long
- Bar-B-Q mate
- Basting brush
- Serving spoon
- Slotted serving spoon
- Peelers
- Egg flip
- Flat grater
- Can opener with bottle opener
- Swiss army knife – with cork screw
- Flat strainer
- Egg rings

- 1 large sharp knife
- 1 bread knife
- Cutting board
- Mesh toaster
- General purpose scissors
- Measuring spoon or a tablespoon
- Extra plate and bowl for serving
- Teaspoons

Personal eating equipment

- Plate
- Bowl
- Mug
- Fork
- Spoon
- Knife
- Steak knife

Cleaning equipment

- Plastic bags
- Wash up bucket
- Container of detergent
- Scourer – the non scratch ones are good
- Cloths
- Dish brush
- Tea towels

cooking fires and coals

making your cooking fire

You can build an above ground fire or you can dig a trench or pit for a pit fire. Pit fires have some advantages over above ground fires such as not being effected as much by wind, being safer in windy conditions and also tending to radiate heat better—especially if using poor quality wood. However, it may be difficult or near impossible to dig a pit or trench if your fire is situated on hard, rocky ground. Either way you should clear the area of combustible material such as leaves, dried grass and twigs for at least three metres around your fire site.

Some people place rocks around the perimeter of the fire to act as a barrier. The problem here is that the rocks tend to get in the way and are easily tripped on   not very safe near a fire. If you do use rocks as a fire ring never use rounded river stones. These are prone to exploding, sending razor sharp fragments of rock flying in all directions when subjected to the intense heat of a camp fire.

Another point worth remembering is that many campsites, and especially the more popular ones, are usually devoid of wood for a fire. It is best to collect a good supply of firewood well before reaching your campsite or, if you have room, bring some from home.

Never cut down trees, either living or dead — always collect fallen wood for your fire. Avoid collecting logs that are hollow as these are often home to small animals and lizards.

Heavy, dense hardwoods such as red gum, ironbark, blue gum, stringy-bark and similar eucalyptus are slow burning and will produce good cooking coals. In the western and outback areas mulga, gidgee and desert oak also produce excellent coals. Gidgee and red gum are favourites of ours as they too produce reliable coals for cooking. Softwoods like pine aren't suitable for cooking fires as they do not produce very good coals, mostly burning to ash.

If you have room, it is a good idea to carry a bag or two of 'heat beads' or barbeque briquettes. These compressed lumps of coal can be used to supplement the coals from your cooking fire, and are especially handy when camp oven cooking with firewood which is less than ideal, such as that found in the high country areas. They provide a reliable, constant heat for up to an hour or more and burn leaving a small pile of ash.

It's also a handy idea to take along a packet of commercial firelighters which you can get at supermarkets. These make lighting a fire much easier than using paper, especially when the wood is damp. Never use petrol to light a fire.

getting ready to cook

Try to start your fire at least 30 minutes, or better still, an hour or so prior to cooking. You will find that the best cooking fire is one with low flame and plenty of glowing coals and this takes time. You can't build a good cooking fire in ten minutes!

For most camp oven cooking you will need a main fire from which to produce coals and a level area a short distance away from this for your coal bed. Some people place aluminium foil on the ground before placing the coals on the coal bed near the main fire. This helps to reduce heat loss from the coals on the cold ground. If you are using a trench fire move the required amount of coals to one end of the trench. If you are barbecuing, grilling or frying wait until the main fire has produced a good bed of coals and place your grate or plate directly over these.

Different cooking styles will use different parts of the fire:

*   Barbecuing, boiling and frying – over direct flame

*   Roasting, stewing and grilling – use red embers and coals

*   Coal cooking – use grey embers. Wrap food in aluminium foil and bury in the grey embers.

For hints on successful cooking in your camp oven see using your camp oven on page 90.

windy weather

Wind can be a real nuisance for the bush cook. Besides blowing dust and grit around and covering everything you cook on the fire with ash, strong winds also make it more difficult to control the heat of your cooking fire by fanning the coals and creating 'hot spots'.

When setting up your bush kitchen take note of any prevailing wind and use natural protection such as trees and large boulders if possible. At times you may need to use your food boxes or whatever is available to form a windbreak. A strategically placed vehicle can also act as an effective windbreak. Do not cut down any living vegetation to use as a windbreak.

equipment suppliers

The cooking gear featured throughout this book is all top quality, that with care will last for many years. Much of it is Australian made and is available from camping and outdoor stores or by mail order from the manufacturers.

Auspit
Rhett Thompson
PMT Leisure Pty Ltd
PO Box 451, Pakenham Vic 3810
Tel: 03 5941 3949
Web: www.auspit.com

Aussie Porta Spits
Darren Brooks
PO Box 23, Hackham SA 5163
Tel: 08 8327 3559 Fax: 08 8327 4466
Mobile: 0417 089 091
Web: www.aussieportaspits.com.au

Bedourie Camp Ovens
Southern Metal Spinners
2 Piping Lane, Lonsdale SA 5160
Tel: 08 8382 6990 Fax: 08 8326 1369
Web: www.southernmetalspinners.com.au

Biji Barbi
Tony Upton
PO Box 110, Hillston NSW 2675
Tel/Fax: 02 6967 2417
Web: www.biji-barbi.com.au

Eco Billy
Rod Dun
Rods Country Camping
Mobile: 0418 423 610
Web: www.ecobilly.com

Furphy Foundry
Drummond Road, Shepparton Vic 3630
Tel: 03 5831 2777 Fax: 03 5831 2681
Web: www.furphyfoundry.com.au

Hillbilly Camping Gear
Mick Mills
21A Kevin Avenue, Ferntree Gully, Vic 3156
Tel: 0407 540 005
Web: www.campingwithhillbilly.com

Nipper Kipper Smoke Ovens
Trevor Dixon
73 Karraschs Road, Craignish Qld 4655
Tel: 07 4128 6491 Fax: 07 4128 6381
Web: www.smokeovens.com

Togar Ovens
Graham Joshua
PO Box 660, Beenleigh Qld 4207
Tel/Fax: 07 5580 1050
Web: www.togarovens.com

Dingo Bush Kettle
Doug Hill
7 Fairmont Street, Boolarra Vic 3870
Mobile: 0427 648 332
Web: www.bushkettle.com.au

Davids' Campfire Cooking
David Ubrihien
PO Box 57, Bega NSW 2550
Tel: 0415 808 236
Web: thebegavalley.org.au/campfirecooking.html

breakfast

The most important meal of the day! Breakfast while camping is often a much more leisurely affair than the rushed 'scoff down a bite while rushing out the door' scenario of our working weekdays. Why not use this extra time to whip up one of these beaut breakfasts that are sure to get you off to a great start.

mick's mini omelettes

mick's mini omelettes

 Cooking time: around 15 minutes
SERVES 2-3

4 eggs
½ onion, finely diced
½ capsicum, finely diced
Milk – a few drops per egg
Salt and pepper to taste

Heat barbecue plate or frying pan. Beat together eggs, onion, capsicum, milk and seasoning. Spoon mixture into greased egg rings. Cook approximately 1 minute – turn and cook other side.

*Tip ~ **These omelettes are great served with sausages or bacon or whack them on toasted muffins – beautiful!***

potato omelette

 Cooking time: around 30 minutes
SERVES 2

4 bacon rashers, diced
2 medium potatoes, peeled and thinly sliced
4 shallots, sliced
1 tablespoon dried mixed herbs
Tabasco sauce to taste
4 eggs, beaten

Cook the bacon in hot oil in frying pan until crisp, remove. Add potatoes, shallots, herbs and Tabasco to pan. Cook until potatoes are just tender, around 20 minutes, carefully stirring a couple of times. Add milk to beaten eggs – mix well. Pour eggs and milk over potato mixture. Cover and cook until eggs are set.

*Tip ~ **Serve sliced with bacon sprinkled on top. This dish is great served at breakfast or even for lunch.***

mud pirates eggs

mud pirates eggs

A mud pirate was just one of a number of terms given to the river boatmen of the Murray-Darling rivers during the days of paddle-steamers. So on your next adventure to the Murray River why not cook up a brekkie of mud pirates eggs.

 Cooking time: around 5-10 minutes

INGREDIENTS PER PERSON
1 egg
1 slice of bread

Butter bread on both sides and cut a hole in the middle. Keep centre. Place bread on barbecue plate or in frying pan. Break egg into each hole and cook till firm on the bottom. Carefully flip over and cook other side. Serve with the fried bread cut out on top of egg.

*Tip ~ **Serve by themselves or with bacon, sausage and fried mushrooms.***

beardies potato cakes

Cooking time: around 10-15 minutes
SERVES 4-6

4 potatoes, grated
1 onion, grated
4 tablespoons plain flour
2 eggs
Salt and pepper to taste

Squeeze liquid out of grated potatoes and onion. Combine all ingredients. Drop small spoonfuls into hot oil on barbecue plate or in frying pan. Cook until well browned on both sides.

*Tip ~ **These potato cakes are delicious served by themselves or as part of a big breakfast fry up with bacon and eggs. For those who like to turn up the heat a friend of ours serves these with a sliced jalepeno chilli pressed in the middle of the potato cake.***

bushman's toast

bushman's toast

 Cooking time: around 5 minutes
SERVES 4

2 eggs
3 tablespoons milk
4 slices of bread
Butter for frying

Beat eggs and add milk. Dip bread in mixture then fry on both sides until golden brown. Serve with bacon or with maple syrup.

*Tip ~ **For a sweeter option use fruit or raisin bread.***

brekkie jaffle

 Cooking time: around 5 minutes
SERVES 1

2 pieces of bread – buttered on the outside
Bacon or ham
1 egg

Place one piece of bread in the jaffle iron with the buttered side down. Lay in the bacon or ham, break the egg over the bacon, season with salt and pepper. Cover with second piece of bread, buttered side out and then close up jaffle iron. Cook jaffle over coals until cooked through.

simple bircher muesli

SERVES 2-3

1 ½ cups of porridge oats
½ cup skim milk
50 g low fat plain yoghurt
50 ml juice – choose your favourite

Mix all ingredients together, cover and refrigerate overnight. In the morning serve with extra yoghurt and fruit of choice with a drizzle of honey.

basic pancake mix

Cooking time: around 5-10 minutes

MAKES 8-10 PANCAKES

1 cup self raising flour
Pinch of salt
1 egg
1 cup milk

Combine flour, pinch of salt and egg. Gradually add milk and beat until smooth. Leave to stand for 1 hour. Heat frying pan and lightly rub with butter. Pour 2 to 3 tablespoons of batter into frying pan tilting pan until batter is evenly distributed. Cook until bubbles appear, flip over and cook second side. Serve with butter and golden or maple syrup; fresh lemon juice and sugar; or our favourite with fresh fruit, yoghurt and golden syrup.

pancakes

no trouble bubble & squeak

 Cooking time: around 10 minutes

Left over cooked mashed potatoes
Left over cooked vegetables

Mix left over mash and vegetables together. Season with salt and pepper. Heat oil or butter in frying pan or on barbecue plate. Place vegetable mix in oil and flatten out. Cook until browned then turn over and brown other side. Don't worry if they break up. Serve with bacon and eggs for a filling breakfast.

bullockies sausage & beans breakfast

During the early days of settlement most heavy transport such as wagons and log jinkers where hauled by bullock teams driven by bullock drivers, or 'bullockies'. Bullocks were stronger than horses, but slower. Driving bullock teams with heavy loads of wool bales or other supplies was hard, physical work. This satisfying breakfast will give you the stamina for your day ahead.

Cooking time: around 30 minutes
SERVES 4

Allow 2 thick sausages per person
Oil
2 large onions, chopped
1 x 420 g tin tomatoes, crushed
1 x 420 g tin baked beans in tomato sauce
2 tablespoons tomato paste

Cook sausages in frying pan or on barbecue plate. Drain on paper towels. Heat oil in frying pan and cook onions until soft. Add tomatoes, baked beans and tomato paste. Bring to the boil and simmer for 5 minutes. Stir occasionally to stop sticking, add water if necessary. Return sausages to pan and heat through.

*Tip ~ **For some extra flavour add a dash of Tabasco or Worcestershire sauce.***

bullockies sausage & beans

barbecues & grilling

The good ol' barbie is often the basis of most outdoor cooking while camping. These barbecue and grilling recipes are sure to take the humble chops and snags to mouth-watering new heights around the camp fire.

30 minute leg of lamb

30 minute leg of lamb

Never thought it was possible to cook a leg of lamb in half an hour? Butterflied legs of lamb, basically a boned out leg roast, are now readily available at butchers and supermarkets. Otherwise ask your butcher to do this for you or you can easily do it yourself. Often they come cryovaced, which greatly extends their keeping time.

 Cooking time: around 30 minutes

SERVES 4

Butterflied lamb leg – one leg will roughly serve 4 hungry campers
Marinade – purchase the lamb already marinated or use one of the marinades from the marinade section of this book

Slowly cook lamb over hot coals on a grill until cooked to your liking.

snagger's chutney chops

You don't have to be a 'rough' shearer to enjoy these delicious lamb chops.

Cooking time: around 15-20 minutes
SERVES 4

8 lamb chops
1 x small jar of fruit chutney
2 teaspoons of curry powder
Oil

Combine chutney with curry powder. Add a dash of oil and mix well. Dip lamb chops into chutney mix then barbecue on heated grill or barbecue plate.

chilli pork chops

Cooking time: around 10-15 minutes

SERVES 6

6-8 pork chops
Oil
1 large onion, chopped
1 garlic clove, crushed
½ cup chilli sauce
¼ cup beer
Couple splashes of Tabasco sauce

In small saucepan or frying pan cook onion and garlic in hot oil until tender. Add chilli sauce, beer and Tabasco sauce. Bring to the boil and remove from heat. Barbecue chops on oiled barbecue plate or grill, brushing chops with sauce whilst cooking. Serve chops with any remaining sauce heated through.

glazed pork chops

Cooking time: around 10-15 minutes

SERVES 4

4 pork chops
⅓ cup apricot jam
1 packet French Onion Soup Mix
Juice of 1 orange

Mix the jam, orange juice and soup mix together. Brush glaze over pork chops. Cook chops on barbecue plate or grill, brushing with glaze whilst cooking. Serve glazed chops with green salad.

garlic steak

 Cooking time: 10 minutes
SERVES 4

4 steaks
1 garlic clove, crushed
1 teaspoon curry powder
½ cup red wine

Combine garlic, curry powder and red wine in a dish. Place steak in marinade, cover and leave for at least an hour. Drain meat, reserving the marinade. Barbecue steak over hot coals on lightly oiled hot plate or grill, brushing with marinade until cooked to your liking.

backblock's spicy steaks

Cooking time: around 5-15 minutes
SERVES 4

4 steaks
2 tablespoons oil
1 onion, finely chopped
3 tablespoons Worcestershire sauce
2 tablespoons tomato sauce
Juice of 1 lemon
1 tablespoon paprika

Mix together oil, onion, sauces, lemon juice and paprika. Add meat and marinate for at least one hour prior to cooking. Brush grill or barbecue plate with oil and cook meat over hot coals, brushing with marinade whilst cooking.

ringers' steak & onion

Ringers are either stockmen or a champion shearer — usually the 'gun' shearer who shears the highest tally of sheep in the shed over a given period.

Cooking time: around 5-15 minutes
SERVES 4

4 steaks – go for the best cuts like fillet, porterhouse or rump
Can of beer, ¼ cup reserved
2 tablespoons Worcestershire sauce
1 large onion, sliced
1 capsicum, sliced
2 garlic cloves, crushed
Butter

Combine ¼ cup beer and Worcestershire sauce, brush over steak. Barbecue steak over hot coals, brushing with sauce whilst cooking. (While steaks are cooking you may as well finish off the rest of the beer!) Meanwhile on barbecue plate or in frying pan, melt butter and cook onion, capsicum and garlic until tender. Serve steak with vegetables on top.

ringers' steak & onion

tandoori lamb cutlets

tandoori lamb cutlets

 Cooking time: around 10-15 minutes

Lamb cutlets, 2-3 per person depending on size
Natural yoghurt (1 small tub per 2 people)
Splash of oil
Indian Tandoori Marinade,
either sauce or powder

Mix yoghurt and Tandoori marinade together - enough for your tastes. We generally use about half a packet or quarter of a bottle. Add a splash of oil and mix well. Thoroughly coat lamb cutlets with mix and leave to marinate. Barbecue cutlets on well-oiled barbecue plate or grill over hot coals until cooked. Serve with green salad or with the couscous salad on page 160.

cobbler lamb chops & red wine

Cooking time: around 15-20 minutes
SERVES 4

8 lamb forequarter chops
1 clove garlic, crushed
2 tablespoons butter
2 carrots, cut into strips
6 mushrooms, sliced
2 onions, chopped
2 tablespoons tomato paste
2 tablespoons red wine
Salt and pepper to taste

Cook lamb chops on oiled barbecue or grill. While chops are cooking, melt butter in a small saucepan, add garlic and vegetables and cook until tender. Add tomato paste, wine and seasonings. Cook until well mixed and heated through. Serve chops with sauce on top.

chicken satay sticks

Cooking time: around 15 minutes

SERVES 2

2 chicken breasts, cut into strips
1 bottle/tin of satay sauce

Thread chicken strips onto skewers (see tip below about skewers). Cook on well oiled barbecue plate or grill. Brush with satay sauce while cooking.

beef, pineapple & capsicum kebabs

Cooking time: around 15 minutes

SERVES 3-4

500 g rump steak, cubed
1 tin pineapple cubes
1 red capsicum, cubed

MARINADE
1 cup chicken stock
¼ cup honey
⅓ cup tomato sauce
1 garlic clove, crushed
2 tablespoons soy sauce
½ teaspoon chilli powder
Ground black pepper to taste

Alternatively thread beef, pineapple and capsicum onto skewers and place in shallow dish. Combine all marinade ingredients and pour over kebabs. Leave for an hour. Barbecue on well oiled barbecue plate or grill until cooked. Brush with reserved marinade whilst cooking.

Tip ~ If using bamboo skewers, soak in water for 30 minutes prior to using to stop skewers burning whilst cooking.

beef, pineapple & capsicum kebabs

old stockmans hut, culgoa floodplain national park

bbq chicken wings

 Cooking time: around 15-20 minutes

1 KG OF CHICKEN WINGS WILL GIVE YOU AROUND 12 WINGS

MARINADE
2 tablespoons each of:
tomato sauce
BBQ sauce
honey
¼ cup white wine (or even beer)
Dash Tabasco sauce

Combine all marinade ingredients. Cover chicken wings with marinade and leave until required (at least one hour). Barbecue wings on oiled hotplate or grill until cooked through and well browned. The wings can be left whole or you can cut them in half at the joint.

Tip ~ For other marinade flavours see the marinades, bastes & sauces on page 225.

bbq pork spare ribs

 Cooking time: around 20 minutes

SERVES 4

1 kg pork spare ribs
¼ cup oil
1 tablespoon lemon juice
1 tablespoon Worcestershire sauce
1 garlic clove, crushed
1 tablespoon brown sugar
½ teaspoon dry mustard
¼ cup fruit chutney

Combine marinade ingredients and mix well. Brush mixture all over ribs and let stand for several hour. Barbecue ribs until golden brown and cooked through, basting with marinade during cooking.

Tip ~ Try one of the other marinades as detailed in the marinades, bastes & sauces on page 225.

bbq corn on the cob

 Cooking time: around 30 minutes

1 corn cob per person
Butter

If using fresh corn, remove silks from corn, but leave husks on. Spread butter over corn cob. Wrap each cob in foil and barbecue for about 30 minutes until tender. Be sure to turn often to avoid burning.

Tip ~ Add one of the following to the butter for additional flavour: crushed garlic, dried herbs, crushed chilli or chilli powder.

bbq corn on the cob

rissoles

The ever popular rissole, along with the snag, would most certainly be favourite barbeque fare to have while camping. We have included a few different flavours here for you to try, making a change from the plain old run-of -the-mill beef variety. Rissoles can be served by themselves with salad or vegetables, or served on fresh bread or buns as burgers with salad and your favourite sauce. After shaping your rissoles it is best for them to be refrigerated for a while prior to cooking. Great on the barbeque, these rissoles can also be cooked in a frying pan.

tex mex burgers

Cooking time: around 15 minutes

MAKES 4 LARGE RISSOLES

500 g beef mince
1 small onion, finely chopped
1 small green capsicum, finely chopped
2 tablespoons of salsa or taco sauce
1 crushed garlic clove
Oil

Combine mince, onion, capsicum, garlic and salsa sauce. Season with salt and pepper to taste. Shape into four large burgers and place in fridge for a while. Cook burgers on lightly oiled barbecue plate. Serve burgers in warmed tortillas with avocado, tomato, lettuce and extra salsa or taco sauce.

herbed beef rissoles

Cooking time: around 15 minutes

MAKES 6 LARGE RISSOLES

1 kg beef mince
1 teaspoon of each: dried thyme dried rosemary dried basil
¼ cup sour cream

Mix all ingredients together thoroughly and divide into 6 equal size rissoles. Refrigerate if possible until ready to cook. Cook rissoles on lightly oiled barbcue plate.

chicken burgers

 Cooking time: around 15 minutes

MAKES 4 RISSOLES

500 g chicken mince
½ cup dried breadcrumbs
1 garlic clove, crushed
2 tablespoons lemon juice
1 egg
Salt and pepper to taste

Combine all ingredients in a bowl and mix well. Using wet hands shape into 4 rissoles. Cook on oiled barbecue plate.

*Tip ~ **These are delicious served on lightly toasted buns as a burger with salad and satay sauce or mango chutney or sweet chilli sauce.***

chicken burger

fish

Australia's most popular recreational pastime, fishing is a well practised activity by campers. Whether you're camped beside the ocean or an inland river, why not drop in a line and see if you can hook yourself something for dinner. And if you manage to land a 'big one' why not try one of the following recipes.

Hints for barbecuing fish

• For best results when barbecuing fish, cook over a bed of hot coals – do not cook over open flame. Heat beads also work well when barbequing fish.

• Fillets and cutlets should be marinated to add flavour and help keep the flesh moist. It's a good idea to baste while cooking with marinade to stop fish drying out.

• Fillets and cutlets should be placed on a well greased barbecue plate or grill. You can also cook the fish on a sheet of greaseproof paper placed directly on the barbeque plate, this stops the flesh from sticking to the plate and tearing.

• Large whole fish can be wrapped in greased foil, with the gut cavity stuffed with herbs and lemon or orange slices for extra flavour.

beer drinkers' trout

 Cooking time: around 10-15 minutes

INGREDIENTS PER PERSON

1 trout
1 bacon rasher
Butter
1 can/stubbie of beer

Gut, scale and clean trout. Rub inside of trout with butter and fold bacon inside. Rub outside of trout with butter. Place trout onto foil. Ensure foil is doubled. Splash some beer in and wrap foil around trout, ensuring that parcel is well sealed. Throw on the barbecue and cook whilst finishing off the beer. Cooking time depends on size of trout.

whole grilled fish

 Cooking time: around 10-15 minutes

INGREDIENTS PER PERSON

1 whole fish per person
Oil
Dried mixed herbs or any other seasoning of choice
Salt & Pepper

Clean and gut fish and make diagonal cuts in both sides of the fish. Brush oil over fish and inside. Season the outside of the fish with salt, pepper and dried mixed herbs. Ensure this is rubbed into the cuts. Place fish in fish cage and grill on both sides until cooked. The skin should be slightly crispy and the flesh firm but moist.

whole grilled fish

cajun prawns

cajun prawns

Cooking time: around 5 minutes

SERVES 4

*1 kg green prawns, peeled and deveined
with tails intact
1 tablespoon vegetable oil
2 tablespoons Cajun seasoning*

Place prawns in a bowl and pour over oil. Sprinkle in the Cajun seasoning and rub all over the prawns. Cook prawns on lightly greased hot barbecue plate until cooked through.

Tip ~ You can cook the prawns in their shell (which is generally our preferred method) or replace the prawns with some firm white fish fillets. These could also be cooked in a large frying pan.

lemon & garlic fish

Cooking time: around 10-15 minutes

SERVES 2

1-2 firm white fish fillets per person

*MARINADE
1 teaspoon lemon rind, grated
½ cup lemon juice
2 tablespoons oil
2 garlic cloves, crushed
2 tablespoons white wine
1 teaspoon sugar
½ teaspoon pepper*

Combine all marinade ingredients in a shallow dish. Add fish cutlets and coat with mixture. Leave to marinate for a couple of hours. Cook fish cutlets on lightly greased hot barbecue plate until tender.

chapter 5

frying pan cooking

A frying pan of some description is a valuable asset to your bush cooking equipment. Try out a few of these recipes in the frying pan and you'll never leave home without one again.

hawkers' mince

hawkers' mince

In the days before online internet shopping, and even before mail order catalogues become commonplace, many remote rural and outback towns and stations where visited by hawkers. These travelling salesmen, who would generally travel around the backblocks by horse and wagon, would have all matter of wares to sell, including everything from pots and pans to lotions and potions. On many outback stations the hawker's visit was looked forward to, as it was often the only opportunity to purchase goods.

 Cooking time: around 20-25 minutes

SERVES 4

750 g beef mince
1 onion, chopped
1 capsicum, chopped
1 garlic clove, crushed
¾ teaspoon mustard powder
¼ teaspoon cayenne pepper
2-3 potatoes cubed, boiled but slightly firm

Heat oil in frying pan. Cook onion and capsicum until tender. Add mince and brown. Add mustard powder, cayenne pepper and salt and pepper to taste. Mix well. Carefully stir in potatoes and heat through, approximately 10 minutes.

Tip ~ This is a quick and easy meal to prepare, the mustard powder and cayenne pepper adding a bite to the mince. You can serve this with your favourite sauce for additional flavour.

simple spaghetti bolognaise

Cooking time: around 20-25 minutes

SERVES 4

500 g beef mince
Crushed garlic to taste
1 onion, chopped
1 capsicum, chopped
420 g tin crushed tomatoes
140 g tub tomato paste
Beef stock cube
Dash Worcestershire sauce
Sliced black olives
Dried Italian herbs, to taste

Gently fry onion, capsicum and garlic in oil in large frying pan. Add mince and brown. Add crushed tomatoes, tomato paste and beef stock cube. Add a dash of Worcestershire sauce, olives and sprinkle of herbs. Bring to the boil then simmer over low heat for 10-15 minutes until sauce has thickened. Serve over pasta of choice with parmesan cheese.

Tip ~ Additional vegetables such as mushrooms can be added. If you prefer a sauce with more moisture add some red wine or water and reduce simmer time.

choice chicken curry

choice chicken curry

This tomato based curry is quite mild, but to beef up the zing add a little more curry powder and even a dash of dried chilli powder.

 Cooking time: around 30-40 minutes

SERVES 4

1 kg chicken thighs, diced
Plain flour seasoned with black pepper
1-2 tablespoons curry powder or to taste
2 onions, sliced
2 garlic cloves, crushed
440 g tin crushed tomatoes
1 chicken stock cube
½ cup water

Coat diced chicken with seasoned flour, shake off excess. Brown chicken pieces in oil in large frying pan, remove and drain. Add onions and garlic to frying pan and cook until soft. Add curry powder and stir until fragrant. Return chicken to frying pan with tomatoes, chicken stock cube and water. Bring to the boil, move to lower heat and simmer until chicken is tender. Stir regularly to stop sticking, if necessary add extra water. Serve with boiled rice.

chicken jambalaya

Cooking time: around 40 minutes

SERVES 4

Oil
1½ cups cooked chicken
1 onion, finely chopped
1 cup rice
1 cup vegetables of choice
1 cup tomato puree
1 cup water
½ teaspoon dried basil
1 tablespoon Worcestershire sauce

Heat oil in a large frying pan. Add onion and cook until soft, about 5 minutes. Add rice and vegetables and stir until well combined. Add tomato puree, water, basil and Worcestershire sauce. Mix well and bring to boil. Move to lower heat and simmer covered until rice and vegetables are tender and liquid is absorbed, approximately 30 minutes. Add chicken and season with salt and pepper. Stir well until heated through.

Tip ~ This is a great recipe to use up left over roast or barbecue chicken, otherwise stir fry 2 to 3 diced chicken breasts. For a different flavour add some ham or some spicy sausage.

thai chicken curry

thai chicken curry

 Cooking time: around 20-30 minutes

SERVES 4

Oil
500 g diced chicken
1 tablespoon of curry paste – either red or green
1 large onion, chopped
400 g can coconut-flavoured evaporated milk
1 cup sliced green beans or peas

Heat oil in fry pan, add diced onion and cook until soft. Stir in curry paste and fry for a minute until fragrant. Add diced chicken and quickly stir fry for a minute or two, then add the can of coconutflavoured evaporated milk and reduce heat to a simmer. Simmer until chicken is cooked through, then add green beans or peas and cook until tender. Serve with boiled rice.

Tip ~ If you like your curry hotter, add extra curry paste.

sweet & sour stir fry

Cooking time: around 10-15 minutes

SERVES 4

750 g chicken strips
1 tablespoon cornflour
305 g tin sweet & sour sauce
1 onion, cut in wedges
1 capsicum, sliced
1 carrot, sliced

Coat chicken strips with cornflour, shake off excess. Heat oil in frying pan and quickly stir-fry meat until well browned, remove from pan. Heat extra oil in pan and add vegetables and stir-fry until tender. Return meat to pan with sweet and sour sauce, stir well and heat through. Serve with boiled or fried rice.

Tip ~ Chicken can be replaced with pork or firm fish fillets. Other vegetables that can be added are shallots, celery or even some cucumber with the seeds scooped out.

cath's best fried rice

Cooking time: around 15-20 minutes

SERVES 4

Oil
1-2 cups of cold boiled rice
2 diced bacon rashers, or some diced ham
1 garlic clove, crushed
4 shallots, thinly sliced - or onion if you don't have
2 eggs, beaten
Handful of peas
Lemon pepper seasoning
Soy sauce

Cook rice the night before or at breakfast and keepin fridge or esky until ready to use. Heat oil in frying pan and cook bacon and shallots in a little oil with garlic until tender. Remove from pan and drain on paper towel. Put a little more oil in frying pan and add beaten eggs. Do not stir, move pan around for egg to cook in a thin layer. Cook egg until firm, then slice into strips with knife or egg flip. Remove from pan and drain on paper towel with bacon mixture. Add a little more oil to frying pan and add rice. Heat through. Add bacon, shallots, egg and peas. Mix thoroughly and heat through. Season with lemon pepper and soy sauce to taste. For a real meal, add a tin of drained prawns or other cooked meat such as chicken or pork.

Tip ~ For best results the rice needs to be really dry and well separated. The best way of doing this is to drain the rice well after cooking and spread out on a tray or plates lined with paper towel then placed in the fridge or ice box. When we cook fried rice in the bush we cook the rice the night before, drain it well then spread it out on plates on paper towel to dry whilst we are still up. Then when we go to bed we transfer the rice to a bowl or container lined with paper towel and put it in the fridge ready for the next night.

cath's best fried rice

cameron corner

easy macaroni

Cooking time: around 30 minutes

SERVES 4

12 wings
1 cup macaroni pasta, cooked
1 tablespoon butter
2 tablespoons plain flour
2 teaspoons dry mustard
1½ cups milk
¾ cup grated tasty cheese
1 teaspoon dried mixed herbs

Melt butter in frying pan. Add flour and mustard and stir until mixture bubbles. Remove from heat and gradually stir in milk until well mixed. Return pan to heat and stir until mixture boils and thickens. Add cheese and stir until melted. Add macaroni and herbs and gently stir until well mixed.

*Tip ~ **Drained tuna, salmon or vegetables can be added to this dish.***

noodle cakes

Easy, quick and delicious. Perfect for breakfast, lunch or dinner.

Cooking time: around 15-20 minutes

MAKES 8 NOODLE CAKES

85 g packet of 2-minute noodles
3 eggs, beaten
200 g of meat (try sliced ham, chicken or even a can of drained prawns or try a combination of meats)
½ cup of vegetables, such as finely diced capsicum, diced beans, and drained corn kernels
½ onion, finely chopped
Oil

Cook 2-minute noodles as per packet – add seasoning if you like. Drain and then cool. In a large bowl combine beaten eggs, noodles, meat, vegies and onion. Mix well. Heat oil in frying pan then cook ¼ cupfuls of noodle mixture until egg is set, about 2-3 minutes. Flip noodle cake over and cook for a further 2 minutes until golden and eggs are cooked through.

noodle cakes

dinkum curried snags

Cooking time: around 15-20 minutes
SERVES 4

2-3 sausages per person
2 onions, chopped
1 large apple, peeled and chopped
2 teaspoons curry powder or to taste
Sultanas
2 beef stock cubes
2 cups water
2 teaspoons corn flour

Cook sausages in frying pan until just cooked. Remove and drain. In frying pan cook onion and apple in a little oil until onions are soft. Add curry powder to frying pan and stir. Add beef stock cube and water and bring to the boil. Combine corn flour with a small amount of liquid from the pan and add to the pan. Put frying pan over moderate coals to let sauce simmer. Add sausages, either whole or sliced, and a handful of sultanas. Simmer until heated through and sauce has thickened. Serve with boiled rice or mashed potato.

Tip ~ For a different taste, add some chopped bacon with the onion.

italian veal

Cooking time: around 20-30 minutes
SERVES 4

Oil
4 large veal steaks
500 ml jar of tomato pasta sauce
Cheese – grated or sliced – any cheese will do but mozzarella works best

Heat oil in frying pan and cook veal steaks until browned on both sides. Remove and drain on paper towel. Add pasta sauce to frying pan and bring to the boil. Lay veal steaks in single layer on top of sauce, then top with cheese. Cover and let simmer for about a minute until the cheese melts.

Tip ~ For some extra flavour some bottled chargrilled vegetables can be placed on top of the veal steaks before adding the cheese.

FRYPAN · CORNER

mexican quesadillas

italian veal

spicy sausage casserole

Cooking time: around 20-30 minutes
SERVES 4

Oil
8 thick spicy pork sausages
1 large onion, chopped
800 g tin of diced tomatoes
Good splash of red wine
Mixed herbs

Heat oil in fry pan and cook sausages until brown all over. Remove sausages and keep warm. Add diced onion to frying pan and cook until soft. Return sausages to pan with the tinned tomatoes, a good splash of red wine and some mixed herbs to taste. Cook until the sausages are cooked through and the tomatoes have reduced and thickened. Serve with fresh bread or some creamy mash.

camping beside the darling river

creamy brandy prawns

 Cooking time: around 20-30 minutes

SERVES 4

Oil
6 shallots, sliced
1 kg green prawns, shelled and deveined
4 tomatoes, peeled and chopped
4 tablespoons peas
4 tablespoons sour cream
2 tablespoons brandy or rum
Black pepper

Heat oil in frying pan. Add shallots and prawns, until prawns have just cooked. Add chopped tomatoes and peas. Move to lower heat and add the sour cream and the brandy, stir well and heat through. Add some cracked black pepper and serve on rice.

quick & easy tuna mornay

Cooking time: around 10-15 minutes

SERVES 2-3

2 tablespoons butter
1 large onion, chopped
½ capsicum, chopped
1 tablespoon flour
¾ cup milk
½ cup cream
⅓ cup grated cheese
310 g can corn kernels drained
185 g can tuna, drained
Worcestershire sauce
Salt and pepper to taste

Melt butter in frying pan, add onion and capsicum and fry for 3 minutes. Add flour and stir constantly until well mixed. Slowly add milk and cream, stirring until mixture thickens. Stir in cheese, corn, tuna, a good dash of Worcestershire sauce and salt and pepper to taste. Mix well until heated through. Serve with pasta.

Tip ~ For a sweeter mornay add a small tin of drained crushed pineapple. Alternatively, the mornay can be mixed through the pasta and poured into a tin with additional cheese on top and baked in the camp oven with coals on top until the cheese melts and turns golden brown.

mexican

We both love Mexican food, so we have included a few of our favourite recipes that can be enjoyed in the bush just as much as at home. They may have a few more ingredients and take just slightly longer to prepare but we think that you'll agree that it'll be time well spent!

outback chilli

Cooking time: around 20-30 minutes

SERVES 4

500 g beef mince
1 onion, finely chopped
1 capsicum, finely chopped
1-2 cloves of garlic, crushed
420 g tin of tomato soup
440 g tin red kidney beans, drained
1 beef stock cube
Chilli powder to taste

Fry onion, capsicum and garlic in a little oil in frying pan. Add mince and brown. Add tomato soup, drained red kidney beans, stock cube and chilli powder. Stir to combine all ingredients and simmer for approximately 20 minutes. Delicious served with boiled rice and sour cream

*Tip ~ **To ensure there isn't too much heat when adding chilli, add in small amounts, mix through and leave for a minute before tasting. Add extra if necessary.***

bush-style mexican fajitas

Cooking time: around 15-20 minutes

SERVES 4-6

500 g chicken strips
1 large onion, sliced
1 capsicum, sliced
Packet of Old El Paso Fajita Rub
¼ cup water
Packet tortillas
Taco sauce
TO SERVE:
shredded lettuce, grated cheese, tomato slices, taco sauce and sour cream

Combine Fajita Rub mix with water. Set aside. Heat oil in frying pan. Add onion and capsicum, cook until tender, remove from pan. Add to pan chicken strips and fry until just cooked. Return vegetables to pan along with sauce mix and heat through until chicken and vegetables are well covered with sauce, add extra water if necessary. Meanwhile heat tortillas in foil over coals. Now here comes the fun part. Serve the chicken mixture on the heated tortillas with taco sauce, lettuce, cheese and tomato. Fold tortilla and serve with sour cream.

*Tip ~ **This recipe makes enough for 6-10 tortillas depending on how hungry you are. For something different you could use either beef or if you're near the seaside, prawns, instead of the chicken.***

bush-style mexican fajitas

mexican quesadillas

 Cooking time: around 5-10 minutes

SERVES 2

2 flour tortillas
Taco sauce
Barbecue chicken, meat shredded
2 spring onions, finely chopped
Grated cheese
Sour cream
Paprika

Use a frying pan to fit the tortillas. These are cooked dry, do not oil or grease the frying pan. Heat a dry frying pan. Place one tortilla in pan and spread with taco sauce. Then place shredded chicken, spring onions and grated cheese over sauce, and place second tortilla on top. Cook for about 4 minutes until the bottom tortilla is nicely browned. Here's the tricky bit - place a plate over pan and tip out tortilla. Then slide tortilla back into pan and cook second side until heated through and cheese has melted. Cut into wedges and serve with sour cream and a sprinkle of paprika.

Tip ~ Any type of cooked meat can be used in this dish.

south of the border beef stir fry

Cooking time: around 15-20 minutes

SERVES 4

750 g beef strips
1 packet taco seasoning
1 red onion, sliced
2 capsicums, sliced
4 tomatoes sliced
Coriander leaves, optional

Combine beef strips and taco seasoning. Heat oil in frying pan and cook beef and onion in batches until beef is browned. Remove from frying pan. Stir fry capsicums until tender. Return beef and onion to pan with tomato and 2 tablespoons of chopped coriander leaves, if you have. Cook until heated through. Serve with boiled rice.

Tip ~ Fresh coriander is great in this dish, so if you can get it do so. Use the leftover to cook all your meals with fresh coriander over the next couple of days such as the cous cous salad, thai salad and home made salsa. However, if you don't have or can't get fresh, minced coriander that comes in a tube or jar is a good alternative.

south of the border beef stir fry

mussels & beer

Blue mussels can be found in estuaries along the southern coastline of New South Wales, throughout Victoria, much of South Australia, the south of Western Australia and Tasmania. Unlike oysters, mussels don't adhere as strongly to rocks and can generally easily be twisted off by a gloved hand. We reckon that the best mussels come from Twofold Bay at Eden, but then again we're biased!

mussels & beer

Cooking time: around 10 minutes
SERVES 4

1 kg mussels, cleaned and de-bearded
1 tablespoon olive oil or butter
4 shallots, chopped (use finely diced onion if you don't have)
1 clove of garlic, crushed
375 ml bottle or can of beer

Gently fry shallots and garlic in oil or butter for about a minute. We like to use a mix of both oil and butter. Add the mussels and pour in the beer. Mix thoroughly and put on the lid. Cook over high heat shaking the pan now and then until all the mussels have opened and cooked. Throw away any mussels that didn't open. Spoon mussels and liquid into bowls and serve with fresh bread.

Tip ~ You will need a large frying pan or pot with a lid for this recipe – a camp oven will even do. Chillies can be added to this recipe, just cook up with the shallots and, if you have, coriander or parsley can be sprinkled over the mussels when dished up. Also remember that the better the beer the better the taste, we like to use a nice wheat beer for these.

mussels & beer

freshwater yabbies

yabbie

yabbies

For those lucky enough to catch some yabbies or marron here's a few hints and recipes. How to kill a yabby? There are a few different methods: a) Place the fresh yabby into the freezer to slow down its metabolism until it dies; b) stab the yabby with a sharp knife in the centre of the head just behind the eyes - this is ideal if you wish to BBQ the yabby; c) possibly the most popular way, and more practical if camping when you don't have a freezer is to bring a very large pot (camp oven works well) of water to a rapid boil, plunge the yabby into the boiling water and boil until the yabby turns red. Make sure you don't overcrowd the pot. These hints and the recipes can also be used for crabs.

col watson's chilli yabbies

 Cooking time: around 10 minutes

SERVES 4

1 kg cooked yabby tails
1 garlic clove, crushed
2 teaspoons minced ginger
1 onion, chopped
2 tomatoes cut into wedges
1 teaspoon chilli sauce, such as Tabasco or Piri Piri
2 tablespoons tomato sauce
1 tablespoon soy sauce
½ cup water

Fry garlic, ginger and onion in oil until fragrant. Add tomato wedges, sauces and water, bring to the boil. Boil for 2 minutes. Add cooked yabbies and heat through. Serve with boiled or steamed rice.

yabbies in wine

Cooking time: around 10 minutes

SERVES 4

1 kg cooked yabby tails
1 onion, diced
1 garlic clove, crushed
½ cup white wine
1 cup cream
Ground black pepper

Heat oil in frying pan. Fry onion and garlic until transparent. Add wine and cream and simmer for a 2 minutes. Add yabbies and heat through. Season with ground black pepper. Serve with boiled or steamed rice.

camp oven cooking

Without doubt a camp oven is the quintessential piece of bush cooking equipment. Once you've mastered the art of cooking in a camp oven these recipes will become standard fare on your camping adventures.

using your camp oven

You will get the best results from your camp oven cooking if you follow a few simple tried and tested procedures.

- Place the oven on or over the main fire to get it nice and hot before you place any food inside. A tripod or grate is ideal for this task. By doing this you won't be drawing heat from the coals to heat the oven.

- If you are cooking recipes that require most of the heat to be coming from the top, then make sure that you get the lid of the oven hot also.

- If you are baking or roasting, when the oven is hot place it on a thin bed of coals a little way from the main fire and put in your food. Now place coals on the lid.

- For recipes that require browning, heap coals in the centre of the lid to produce a more concentrated heat.

- Bedourie ovens tend to cook better if they are placed in a shallow hole with coals on the bottom and half buried up the sides with hot ash and embers, and some coals on the lid.

- When baking, place a trivet or cake rack inside your camp oven. This allows the heat to circulate better and helps avoid burning your food on the base of the oven.

- The type of wood you are burning for coals will dictate how often you need to replenish coals under and on the lid of the camp oven.

- Try to minimise how often you remove the lid from your oven. Check on dampers and breads after 20 minutes and roasts after 30-40 minutes. Excessive lifting of the lid allows heat to escape and results in longer cooking times.

- When cleaning, never pour cold water into a hot cast iron oven as it may cause it to crack. Always use warm or hot water.

- Take care not to drop cast iron camp ovens on hard surfaces such as rocks or concrete. Cast iron is brittle and you could easily crack your oven.

camp oven temperatures

To check the temperature in a camp oven place a piece of newspaper or paper towel inside the oven for approximately 5 minutes. Rule of thumb is:

- If paper is black and smoking – the oven is too hot.

- If paper is a light brown to yellow colour – the oven is moderate to hot.

- If paper is a cream or pale yellow colour – the oven is slow to moderate.

When cooking on wet or damp ground you need to allow extra cooking time.

roasting in a camp oven

Cooking a roast in the bush in a camp oven is really no different to cooking one at home. The main difference is you need to check the heat of the coals regularly to ensure your meat is cooking evenly. The best way of doing this is to have plenty of hot coals ready, so each time you check the meat, say every 30-40 minutes, you have some new coals to place on the lid and shovel around the camp oven. A bag of barbeque briquettes can come in handy when your campfire coals aren't fully up to the task!

Cooking times for roasts depend on the size of the meat and the heat of your coals, that's why it's important to check the meat regularly!

1. Ensure camp oven is well oiled. Place oven over fire to get it nice and hot.

2. Place meat in camp oven and cover with lid.

3. Place camp oven in hot coals and shovel coals on lid.

4. Depending on the size of the meat, cook for 1 to 2½ hours.

5. Vegetables cut into serving sizes, eg: potato, pumpkin, sweet potato or onion can be added in the last 40-45 minutes.

6. Before carving, let the meat stand for at least 5-10 minutes for juices to flow out and to firm, keep it warm by covering with aluminium foil.

7. Serve meat with vegetables and gravy/sauce of choice. There is now a large range of instant gravies available that are easy to carry and make by simply adding boiling water to the gravy mix.

When roasting a chicken

1. Remove the neck and any giblets in the cavity, rinse thoroughly and dry with paper towel.

2. Brush melted butter over bird.

3. Roast chicken breast-side up for 15 minutes in camp oven over flame.

4. Turn chicken over and place camp oven on coals and cook for 50-60 minutes.

Chicken is cooked when juices run clear from thigh when pierced with a skewer and when a leg rocks easily in the socket.

seasoning ideas for roasts

Roast lamb

- Rub dried rosemary over the lamb.
- Rub a mixture of crushed garlic and dried rosemary over the lamb.
- Cut slits in the lamb and place whole garlic cloves in.
- A herbed mustard (which can be mixed to a smooth paste and rubbed/ brushed over the leg) made from: 3 tablespoons French mustard, 3 teaspoons soy sauce, 1 clove of garlic,1 teaspoon rosemary and oil.

Roast beef

- Rub a mixture of seeded mustard & red wine over beef.
- Make a spicy rub from: 1 teaspoon ground cumin, ½ teaspoon chilli powder, 2 crushed garlic cloves and ½ teaspoon salt. Combine together and rub into beef, and drizzle some oil over.

Roast chicken

- Rub dried mixed herbs, salt and pepper over bird after brushing with butter.
- Place ½ lemon in cavity with dried oregano or marjoram.
- Place knob of butter, crushed garlic cloves and dried rosemary in cavity.

- Chicken stuffing - Combine 1½ cups of breadcrumbs, one finely chopped celery stick, one finely chopped onion, 1 teaspoon of dried mixed herbs and 1 lightly beaten egg. Fill chicken cavity, do not pack too tightly.

stewing in a camp oven

Stews and casseroles are best cooked with slow to moderate heat and cooked over a long period of time. In most cases the longer, the better as the meat, especially beef and lamb, will tend to be much more succulent and tender with long, slow cooking. An advantage of this slow cooking method allows for the use of cheaper cuts of meat. This is especially handy for travelling on a budget. When stewing in the camp oven get the oven nice and hot by placing it over a hot fire, add meat to brown in the hot oven then add the other ingredients to the oven. The camp oven can then either be set on a light bed of coals or hung over a low fire on a tripod or grate to gently cook.

baking in a camp oven

When baking in your camp oven, it is best to place tins and trays on a trivet. This lifts the cooking tray off the base of the oven, helping to alleviate the problem of having too much concentrated heat on the bottom, allowing the heat inside the camp oven to circulate around the food. Although providing good results when using cast iron camp ovens, this method is almost essential when baking in spun steel ovens, which have thinner bases that conduct heat more quickly.

traveller's stew

traveller's stew

Cooking time: around 1¾ - 2 hours

SERVES 4-6

750 g chuck steak, cubed
¼ cup flour
Oil
2 onions, sliced
2 large potatoes, peeled and thickly sliced
2 carrots, sliced thickly
1 can beer
1 cup beef stock
1 tablespoon soy sauce
2 bay leaves, if you have them

Toss meat in flour, shake off excess. Heat oil in camp oven and brown meat. Remove and drain on paper towels. Place sliced potatoes in bottom of camp oven. Place meat, onions and carrots on top of potatoes. Add some black pepper. Pour in beer, beef stock and soy sauce. Throw in bay leaves if using. Bake in camp oven uncovered on a grill above medium coals until meat is tender, around 1½ to 2 hours. Serve with freshly made damper or fresh bread.

teamster's beef & beans

Cooking time: around 1½ hours

SERVES 4

500 g chuck steak, cubed
1 onion, chopped
2 tablespoons paprika
2 beef stock cubes
¾ cup warm water
420 g can baked beans

Brown beef in camp oven in hot oil. Add onion and cook until soft. Sprinkle paprika over beef and onions. Combine water and stock cubes. Pour over meat and mix well. Cover and cook until meat is tender – 1 to 1½ hours, adding water if needed. When meat is tender add baked beans and cook for further 10-15 minutes. Delicious served with potatoes and bread.

outback beef casserole with dumplings

This is a hearty stew just perfect for those long winter nights sitting around the camp fire in the outback. It cooks very nicely in the camp oven using a shovel full or two of coals from the dense wood found in the outback. We also regularly cook this dish at home in our wood stove during the winter months.

Cooking time: around 2 hours

SERVES 4-6

1 kg chuck steak, cubed
Oil
½ cup seasoned flour
2 medium onions, diced
1 capsicum, diced
2 small carrots, diced
1½ cups beef stock
2 tablespoons Worcestershire sauce
1 tablespoon soy sauce

DUMPLINGS
1 cup self-raising flour
2 tablespoons butter
2-3 tablespoons milk
⅓ cup grated cheddar cheese
1 teaspoon of dried mix herbs - optional

Lightly toss meat in seasoned flour, shake off excess. Heat oil in camp oven and brown meat. Add onions and cook until brown. Combine beef stock, Worcestershire sauce and soy sauce and pour over beef and onions. Cover and cook on medium coals for 1 hour to 1¼ hours. Add capsicum and carrots, bake for further 20-30 minutes until meat is tender. Place dumplings (see recipe below) on top of casserole. Brush dumplings with extra milk. Replace camp oven lid and place coals on top and bake for 15 minutes until dumplings are golden and puffed.
DUMPLINGS
Place flour in bowl. Rub butter into flour using fingers to make a fine crumbly texture. Add milk, cheese and herbs. Mix thoroughly. Place onto floured surface and knead until smooth. Pull apart into rough balls and place dumplings on top of casserole, brush with milk.

simplest beef hot pot

 Cooking time: around 1½ hours

SERVES 4

750 g blade steak, cubed
Oil
1 packet Curry Hot Pot Casserole Base
1½ cups water
410 g tinned tomatoes

Heat oil in camp oven over hot coals and brown meat. Combine Hot Pot Base, water and tomatoes and pour over meat. Cook covered in camp oven until meat is tender, approximately 1½ hours.

black stump casserole

Any place the 'other side of the black stump' was as far away from civilisation as possible. This tasty casserole is one recipe you need to have on hand on your travels beyond the black stump!

   Cooking time: around 2¾ hours

SERVES 4-6

2 kg chuck steak, cubed
4 tablespoons plain flour
4 large onions, sliced
1 can of beer, not cold
2 cloves garlic, crushed
4 teaspoons of brown sugar
2 tablespoons vinegar
1 bay leaf
1 teaspoon dried mixed herbs
Salt and pepper to taste

Coat meat with flour and shake off excess. Heat oil in camp oven and brown meat. Add onions and cook until golden. Add extra oil or butter if necessary. Add garlic, sugar, vinegar, herbs and salt and pepper to taste. Pour in beer and mix well. Cover and cook over medium coals for 2-2½ hours until meat is tender and gravy thick, stirring occasionally.

Tip ~ This casserole is delicious served with potatoes, either mashed or just boiled, or even by itself with some fresh bread to mop up the gravy.

flame'n good curry

The name says it all, this is bush curry at its best.

Cooking time: around 1¼ hours

SERVES 4-6

750 g round steak, cubed
Oil
3 onions, chopped
4 garlic cloves, crushed
1 tablespoon crushed ginger
1 teaspoon chilli powder
2 teaspoons ground cardamon
2 teaspoons turmeric
1½ cups beef stock
6 potatoes, peeled and cubed

Heat oil and brown meat in camp oven. Add onion, garlic and ginger to pan and cook until onion is tender. Stir in chilli powder, cardamon and turmeric and cook until fragrant. Add beef stock and cook covered over medium coals until meat is nearly tender, depending on coals around 30-45 minutes. Add potatoes and cook uncovered until meat and potatoes are tender. Serve with rice.

flame'n good curry

diamantina river, outback queensland

hargrave's reward

 Cooking time: after 1 hour
SERVES 4-6

500 g topside steak, cubed
Oil
3 large carrots, sliced
1 large onion cut into rings
2 tablespoons of Gravox Powder
2 cups water
½ cup of plain flour
Salt and pepper to taste

Heat oil in camp oven over hot coals. Toss steak in flour seasoned with salt and pepper. Cook steak in hot oil until browned. Remove steak and drain excess oil. Add sliced carrot and onion to camp oven and place steak on top. Mix Gravox and water and pour over meat and vegetables. Cook slowly in camp oven until meat is tender, approximately 1 hour. Serve with either boiled or mashed potato and fresh damper.

boss cocky osso bucco

Cooking time: around 2 hours
SERVES 6

1 to 2 osso bucco pieces per person
2 cups plain flour, seasoned
Oil
1 large onion, diced
2 garlic cloves crushed
1 large carrot, sliced
⅔ cup wine, white or red
⅔ cup beef stock
410 g tin crushed tomatoes
¼ cup tomato paste
½ teaspoon sugar

Heat camp oven over hot coals. Coat osso bucco pieces in seasoned flour, shake off excess. Heat oil in camp oven and brown meat, drain on paper towels. Add onion, garlic and carrot to camp oven, cook until onion is soft. Add wine, stock, undrained tomatoes, tomato paste and sugar. Bring to boil then simmer for 5 minutes. Return meat to camp oven, cover and bake in low to medium coals until meat is tender, around 1 hour and 45 minutes.

Tip ~ The slow cooking of this dish makes the meat so tender it just falls off the bone. Boss cocky osso bucco tastes even better reheated the next day!

boss cocky osso bucco

corner country meat loaf

corner country meat loaf

You don't have to head off to the Corner Country to whip up this dinkum meat loaf, but it's an easy, tasty dinner and the leftovers are great on sandwiches the next day.

 Cooking time: around 1 hour
SERVES 6-8

500 g beef mince
1 large onion, chopped
2 cloves garlic, crushed
140 g tub tomato paste
2 tablespoons Worcestershire sauce
1 carrot, grated
1 cup corn kernels
½ cup peas
1 teaspoon mixed herbs
1 egg, beaten
1½ cups breadcrumbs

Combine all ingredients and place into greased loaf tin. If you don't have a loaf tin you can shape this into a loaf and wrap well in foil. Cook in camp oven over medium coals for 1 hour or until cooked through. Drain off excess juices before cutting.

Tip ~ For a change, use different vegetables. Other variations on this basic meat loaf is to line the loaf tin with bacon slices; place a couple of hard boiled eggs down the centre of the loaf prior to cooking; or cover the cooked meat loaf with mashed potato then brush with melted butter and return to camp oven for a further 15 minutes with coals on the lid and cook until browned.

bush echidnas

Cooking time: around 1 hour
SERVES 4

500 g mince
1 onion, finely chopped
1 egg
½ cup uncooked rice
Salt and pepper to taste
Mixed herbs
420 g tin tomato soup
¾ soup tin of water

Combine mince, onion, egg and rice in bowl. Season with salt, pepper and mixed herbs. Mix well. Flour your hands and then shape the mince mixture into small rissoles. Place rissoles in camp oven or dish inside camp oven. Combine tomato soup and ¾ the tin of water, mix well and pour over rissoles. Cover and cook over low heat for an hour until rissoles and rice is cooked through and the sauce is thick. Serve with mashed potato.

Tip ~ Grated carrot can be added to the mince mixture. Extra water may need to be added during the cooking time.

moroccan lamb

Cooking time: around 1hr 10min

SERVES 4

750 g lamb, cubed
Oil
2 cups chicken stock
2 onions, finely chopped
½ cup pitted prunes, halved
½ cup dried apricots, halved
1 teaspoon powdered ginger
1 teaspoon ground cinnamon

Heat oil in camp oven over hot coals. Cook lamb in hot oil until well browned. Add stock, onion, fruit and seasonings to camp oven. Simmer covered until meat is tender, approximately 1 hour. Serve with either boiled rice or couscous and fresh bread.

dee's chow mein

Cooking time: around 30-40 minutes
SERVES 4

500 g mince
1 onion, finely chopped
1 carrot, grated
¼ cabbage, shredded
Handful of rice
1 packet of 2 minute chicken noodles, crushed
Curry powder to taste
Water

Heat oil in camp oven and fry onion until tender. Add mince and brown. Add carrot, cabbage, crushed noodles and rice adding enough water to cover all ingredients. Add the flavour sachet from noodles and curry powder to taste. Allow to simmer until rice and noodles are cooked through. Adding extra water if necessary. Serve with crusty fresh bread or damper and sauce of your choice.

*Tip ~ **Leftovers are tasty cold on sandwiches with tomato sauce.***

dee's chow mein

baked chops with tomatoes

Cooking time: around 1 hour
SERVES 4

4-6 large lamb chops of choice
2 tablespoons oil
3 tablespoons red wine
1 tablespoon dried thyme
Salt and pepper

TOMATO TOPPING
410 g tin crushed tomatoes
1 capsicum, diced
1 red onion, diced
2 crushed garlic cloves

Place chops in deep dish. Mix oil, wine, thyme, salt and pepper together and then pour over chops. Cover and marinate in fridge for 1 hour.
TOMATO TOPPING
Combine crushed tomatoes, capsicum, onion and garlic. Place lamb chops in warmed camp oven, or in dish in camp oven, and spoon tomato topping over. Cook in camp oven in medium to hot coals for 1 hour until chops are cooked through. Serve with mash potato or rice.

baked chops with tomatoes

the block stew

This is a throw together stew that we cook regularly at our bush block in the NSW Monaro region. This is prime sheep country, allowing us easy access to good lamb and mutton, namely the neighbour's deep freeze! When we get low on supplies we visit their deep freeze - then share the stew and a few beers with them.

Cooking time: around 3-4 hours
SERVES 4-6

1½ kg lamb or mutton pieces, either with or without bone
Seasoned flour
2 large onions, diced
2 cloves of crushed garlic
2 medium carrots, sliced – optional
1 or 2 stock cubes – whatever you have on hand
1 can beer – we like to use a flavoursome stout
Lamb seasonings
3 or 4 potatoes diced
Salt and pepper to taste

Toss lamb in flour and shake off excess. Brown meat in hot oil in camp oven in batches until browned, drain on paper towels. Heat extra oil in camp oven and brown onion and garlic. Return meat to camp oven with carrots, stock cubes, a good sprinkling of lamb seasonings and then pour in beer. Cover and cook over low heat until meat is just on tender, add extra liquid if necessary. Add extra lamb seasonings and salt and pepper. Then throw in the potatoes and cook until the meat is really tender and the potatoes are cooked.

Tip ~ Depending on how I feel, if I have meat on the bone I will sometimes take the meat off the bones. This is generally done after about an hour or so of cooking. Just take all the meat out of the camp oven and thoroughly cut all meat off the bone, dice it up and then put back into the camp oven. Some dried peas can also be thrown into the stew for the last 10-15 minutes of cooking.

lamb & mushie stew

lamb & mushie stew

 Cooking time: around 2 hours

SERVES 4

4-6 large lamb leg chops
440 g tin cream of mushroom soup
¼ cup chicken stock
½ cup red wine
250 g button mushrooms, sliced

Trim lamb chops of any excess fat. Heat some oil in camp oven and brown chops, drain on paper towels. Once all chops are browned return to camp oven. Mix together the soup, stock and wine. Pour over chops. Bake in camp oven on medium coals for 1½ hours. Cook mushrooms in a frying pan in a little oil until brown, then stir through the stew. Cook for a further ½ hour or until the meat is tender.

jumbuck stew

A 'jumbuck' is a term once used in the western districts from about the mid 1800s for a young sheep, but also encompassed sheep in general. Even the swaggie in Waltzing Matilda shoved a jumbuck in his tucker bag to cook up for dinner! Although the term 'lamb' is more often used today, most rural people prefer mutton, as it has more flavour.

Cooking time: around 1½ hours

SERVES 4-6

8 medium floury potatoes, peeled and thickly sliced
1 kg lamb chops
4 large onions, thickly sliced
2 cups chicken stock
2 bay leaves
Ground pepper

Trim chops of any excess fat. Arrange half the potato slices in the bottom of heated camp oven, or in a dish to fit in the camp oven. Place meat and onions on top of potatoes, then arrange the balance of potato slices on top. Pour in chicken stock, add bay leaves and ground pepper to taste. Cover and cook with medium heat coals around the camp oven and on the lid for 1½ hours until the chops are tender.

Tip ~ To ensure potatoes do not stick to the base of the camp oven, do not put coals directly under the camp oven. The potatoes will break down during cooking and thicken the stock.

cooee stew

On outback stations chicken was a rare treat, a change from either mutton or beef. So when this flavoursome fare is ready to be dished up and the cooee call goes out, it will have people coming from all directions.

  Cooking time: around 1hr 10 mins

SERVES 6

2 kg chicken pieces
1 large onion, sliced
2 large potatoes, peeled and cut into 2 cm cubes
1 green capsicum, chopped
3 tomatoes, quartered
1½ cups chicken stock
¼ teaspoon cayenne pepper
1½ tablespoons Worcestershire sauce
420 g tin sweetcorn kernels, drained
1 tablespoon plain flour
1 tablespoon melted butter

Brown chicken on all sides in hot oil in camp oven. Remove and drain on paper towel. Cook onion in camp oven until soft. Add potatoes and capsicum. Stir well to mix with onions. Return chicken to camp oven with tomatoes, stock, cayenne pepper and Worcestershire sauce. Bring to the boil, season with salt. Move to medium heat and simmer for 45 to 50 minutes. Add corn and cook for a further 15 minutes until chicken is tender. Mix flour and butter together. Add to the pan gradually, stirring as you go. Add salt and pepper if necessary and cook for further 5 minutes until sauce is thickened.

apricot chicken

 Cooking time: around 40-60 minutes

SERVES 4

8 chicken pieces
¼ cup seasoned flour
1 tablespoon oil
1 onion, sliced
1 packet of French Onion Soup mix
425 ml can apricot nectar
425 g can apricot halves, drained

Toss chicken in seasoned flour, shake off excess. Heat oil in camp oven and quickly cook chicken until browned. Add onion to camp oven and cook until soft. Combine French Onion Soup Mix with apricot nectar, pour over chicken. Cover and bake in medium coals on bottom and top until chicken is cooked, about 40 minutes depending on heat of coals stirring occasionally ensuring that chicken is not sticking to bottom. Stir in apricot halves. Cook uncovered for further 10 minutes until heated through. Serve with rice or potatoes and vegetables if you have.

sundowner's chicken casserole

During the days of swagmen and other itinerant bush workers, this term was coined for those who arrived at a property or station late in the afternoon, often around nightfall. In exchange for a meal most swaggies would chop firewood for the kitchen or undertake other odd jobs as required, however Sundowners, turning up too late to work still often obtained food and shelter for the night. Sundowners usually left early the next morning!

  Cooking time: around 1½ to 2 hours

SERVES 4

8 chicken drumsticks
1 onion, sliced
1 garlic clove, crushed
1 carrot, sliced
1 capsicum, sliced
1 chicken stock cube
¾ cup water
¼ cup red or white wine
410 g tin of crushed tomatoes
1 teaspoon mixed herbs
Salt and pepper

Fry onion, garlic, carrot and capsicum in hot oil for 3-4 minutes in camp oven. Add chicken and brown. Add stock cube, water, wine, tomatoes and herbs. Season with salt and pepper. Cover camp oven and simmer over medium coals for 1½ to 2 hours until chicken is cooked and tender. Serve over pasta or with boiled rice.

fiery thighs

Cooking time: around 1½ hours

Chicken thighs, 1-2 per person
Chicken Dry Rub – refer to rub mix in Spit Roasting section page 139

Heat camp oven over hot coals. Rub a little oil over the chicken thighs, then thoroughly rub the dry rub all over the chicken. Place thighs in the camp oven and cover. Bake in moderate coals around the camp oven and on the lid, until thighs are cooked through. Thighs are cooked when the thickest part is pierced with a skewer and juices run clear.

drumsticks in special sauce

chicken paella

Cooking time: around 30 minutes

SERVES 4

¼ cup plain flour, seasoned with black pepper
2 chicken breasts, cubed
Oil
2 garlic cloves, crushed
1 capsicum, chopped
1 onion, finely chopped
1 zucchini, sliced
1 cup rice
410 g tinned chopped tomatoes
2 cups chicken stock
½ cup peas

Cover chicken in seasoned flour, shake off excess. Cook chicken in oil in camp oven until browned, then remove. Add garlic, onion, capsicum and zucchini to camp oven and cook for 2-3 minutes. Add chopped tomatoes with juice, chicken stock and rice. Bring to boil then simmer with lid on until liquid is absorbed and rice is cooked. Stir in chicken and peas – if using dried peas add prior to all liquid is absorbed. Cook for a further 5 minutes or until warmed through. Add a pinch of dried basil and parsley if available and stir through.

drumsticks in special sauce

Cooking time: around 1½ hours

Chicken drumsticks, 3-4 per person
Tomato sauce
Worcestershire sauce
Garlic - optional

Place drumsticks in camp oven. Mix 3 parts tomato sauce to 1 part Worcestershire sauce. Add garlic if using and slosh sauce over the chicken. Cook in camp oven over medium coals until tender, about 1½ hours.

south coast stew

If you are camping by the coast this is a good recipe to use up some of that extra fresh fish you've caught!

 Cooking time: around 40 minutes
SERVES 4-6

1 kg thick fish fillets, cut into chunks
¼ cup oil
¼ cup plain flour
2 celery sticks, diced
1 onion, diced
1 capsicum, diced
1 tablespoon curry powder
800 g tin tomatoes
¼ cup water
2 teaspoon sugar
Salt and pepper to taste

Heat oil in camp oven and stir in flour. Cook, stirring frequently, until flour turns a dark brown and mixture has thickened. Add celery, onion and capsicum. Cook until tender. Add curry powder and cook for 1 minute. Add tomatoes and their liquid, water, sugar and salt. Bring to boil. Move to low heat and add fish chunks. Bake over low heat for 20-30 minutes, until fish flakes easily with a fork.

*Tip ~ **For a variation halve the quantity of fish and add 500 g of uncooked prawns to this dish.***

easy minestrone soup

 Cooking time: around 20 minutes
SERVES 4

1 tablespoon oil
1 onion, finely chopped
1 capsicum, chopped
140 g tub tomato paste
4 cups water
1 vegetable stock cube
1 tablespoon Italian herbs
½ cup small pasta
440 g can mixed vegetables
310 g can butter beans

Heat oil in camp oven over hot coals. Add onion and capsicum and cook until tender. Add next five ingredients and bring to the boil. Place oven on grate over coals and simmer away for 15 minutes until pasta is just cooked. Add drained tins of mixed vegetables and butter beans and heat through.

*Tip ~ **This quick and easy soup is delicious served with some crusty bread or freshly made damper on a cold winter's day for lunch or dinner.***

underground mutton casserole

  Cooking time: around 1¾ hours

SERVES 4-6

1 rabbit cut into 6-8 pieces
2 tablespoons flour seasoned with salt and pepper
1 onion, sliced
4 bacon rashers, chopped
1 cup tinned peas
1 carrot, sliced
1 packet chicken noodle soup
3 cups water

Cover rabbit pieces with seasoned flour, shake off excess. Fry onion and bacon in oil or butter in camp oven until tender. Add rabbit, drained peas, carrot and chicken noddle soup to camp oven. Pour over water. Bake in camp oven until rabbit is cooked, about 1 to 1½ hours

bush sausage rolls

Cooking time: around 30 minutes

SERVES 4-6

250 g mince –either
sausage or beef
1 onion, diced
Sauce of choice
Herbs and spices
Dry breadcrumbs
Puff pastry, see page 213

Fry the mince and onion in a frying pan until the mince is browned. Add a squirt of your favourite sauce and then some herbs and spices to taste. Slightly cool mixture. At this point if the mixture is too wet add in some dry breadcrumbs. Roll out puff pastry on floured board until thin. Place quantity of mince mixture on pastry, roll up then cut off. Repeat till mince and pastry is used up. Press ends of the roll down and then place sausage rolls on well greased tray. Prick tops and brush with milk. Place on tray and then put on a trivet in hot camp oven and bake with moderate coals on the base and on the lid until pastry is slightly puffed and golden.

Tip ~ Or the cheats way, roll up saveloys or even frankfurts in the pastry.

ubirr rock, kakadu national park

camp oven pizza

Pizzas in the camp oven are easy to make. You have the choice of using home made pizza bases (see page 212 for Pizza Dough recipe), using pita or Lebanese bread or store bought pizza bases. If you don't have any pizza sauce then tomato paste is a good replacement. Add in some mixed herbs or some oregano and garlic and spread over the base.

Cooking time: around 10-15 minutes

Pizza base
Pizza sauce
Grated mozzarella cheese
Toppings of choice
Herbs and spices

Cover pizza base with pizza sauce, toppings and cheese. Place prepared pizza on a tray and place on trivet in camp oven. Place most of the hot coals on the lid and only a small amount under the camp oven and cook until the pizza base is crispy and your pizza topping has heated through and the cheese is golden.

Tip ~ If you don't have a camp oven, pizzas can be made just as easily in a heavy based frying pan. Place the prepared pizza into a greased frying pan and cover with the lid or aluminium foil. To ensure that the base does not burn place pan over low coals or on a grate above coals.

satay chicken & banana pizza

satay chicken & banana pizza

This is one of our favourite pizzas! However, many people question the combination of satay chicken and banana. All we can say is: don't knock it 'til you've tried it!

 Cooking time: around 10-15 minutes

SERVES 2-3

Chicken breast or thighs, cut into strips
1 bottle or tin of satay sauce
Pizza base
Pizza sauce
Banana, sliced
Mushrooms, sliced
Onion, sliced
Grated mozzarella or other pizza cheese

Fry chicken strips in oil until cooked. Remove from heat and drain off any liquid. Pour satay sauce over chicken until well coated. Mix a little satay sauce with pizza sauce. Spread pizza base with pizza/satay sauce. Sprinkle thin layer of grated cheese over sauce. Arrange onion, mushrooms, banana and cooked chicken on top. Sprinkle with more cheese. Bake in camp oven until base is crispy and cheese has melted and turned golden brown.

stockman's egg & bacon pie

 Cooking time: around 30 minutes

SERVES 3-4

4 eggs, beaten
½ cup self-raising flour
1½ cups milk
4 bacon rashers, chopped
1 cup grated cheese
1 onion, finely diced

Combine beaten eggs, milk and flour. Mix well. Add bacon, cheese and onion. Season with salt and pepper and pour mixture into greased pie plate. Place on trivet in camp oven, then place camp oven in a hollow in the ground with moderate coals under the base and around the sides, and with hot coals on top. Bake until set.

*Tip ~ **This could even be cooked up for a filling and tasty breakfast.***

stockman's egg and bacon pie

spuds in their jackets

 Cooking time: around 30-45 minutes

PER PERSON
Potato
Oil
Filling of choice

SUGGESTED TOPPINGS/ FILLINGS
Butter and cracked black pepper
Sour cream and chives
Grated cheese with finely chopped ham/bacon
and chopped spring onions
Mushrooms in butter
Heated left overs
Left over Outback Chilli or Bolognaise Sauce
Heated creamed corn
Heated baked beans

Pierce potatoes all over with a fork and rub with oil. Place in well-oiled camp oven, cover and place in medium to hot coals on base and lid. Cook potatoes for 30-45 minutes. Remove from camp oven. Cut a cross in the top of the potato and squeeze the sides to open out. Top with your favourite topping/filling.

Tip ~ For those that don't have a camp oven, pierce potatoes all over with a fork, rub with oil and wrap in aluminium foil. Place potatoes in the camp fire coals for about 1½ to 2 hours until cooked.

nachos

This recipe is great for a snack with a couple of beers around the camp fire, or jazzed up and eaten as meal on its own.

Cooking time: around 10 minutes

Corn chips
Grated cheese
Chilli powder
Salsa or taco sauce
Avocado dip
Sour cream

Spread a layer of corn chips on a foil lined baking tray then sprinkle with grated cheese and a little chilli powder. Spread either salsa or taco sauce over the top. Sprinkle more grated cheese over the top. Place in camp oven on trivet and bake with hot coals on base and on lid until heated through and cheese melts. Serve topped with avocado dip and sour cream.

Tip ~ Refried beans can also be added.

spuds in their jackets

cheats bush sausage rolls

nachos

stuffed pumkin

stuffed pumpkin

  Cooking time: around 2 hours

SERVES 6-8

1 large pumpkin
3-4 cups cooked rice
3 cooked bacon rashers, chopped
6 spring onions, chopped
2-3 tomatoes, chopped
Mixed herbs to taste
Salt and pepper
¼ cup chicken stock

Place pumpkin in foil lined camp oven. Bake over moderate coals until tender, approximately 1 hour. Remove from oven and allow to cool. Carefully cut top off pumpkin and remove seeds, do not remove flesh. Combine rice, bacon, spring onions, tomatoes, herbs, salt and pepper to taste. Mix well and spoon mixture into pumpkin shell. Return pumpkin to camp oven. Pour chicken stock over pumpkin filling and replace pumpkin top. Place camp oven over coals and cook for 30 minutes or until filling is hot and pumpkin flesh is completely cooked.

Tip ~ Individual golden nugget pumpkins could be used.

selector's potato & mushie bake

Cooking time: around 30-40 minutes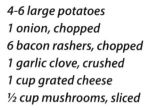

SERVES 4-6

4-6 large potatoes
1 onion, chopped
6 bacon rashers, chopped
1 garlic clove, crushed
1 cup grated cheese
½ cup mushrooms, sliced

Roughly cut potatoes and boil until just tender,drain. Fry onion and garlic in a little oil or butter until tender. Add chopped bacon and sliced mushrooms andfry until bacon is cooked. Add chopped pottoes and gently mix well. Place in camp oven or dish in camp oven. Sprinkle grated cheese on top.
Bake in camp oven with medium coals on bottom and hot coals on top until cheese is melted and turns golden.

spit roasting

Spit roasting offers an easy and delicious cooking alternative in your camp kitchen. You can expect to get tender, moist, juicy meat. This is due to the direct heat method of cooking and the meat self-basting whilst continually rotating.

Many years ago Craig made a portable spit, which consists of two posts with brackets welded to them, to hold the spit rod and motor. The posts have a tee piece on the top to help with knocking them into the ground with a hammer. The spit rod is a length of stainless steel with a small section of square stainless steel, which fits into the drive of the spit motor, welded to one end.

The spit is powered by a small rotisserie motor that runs on two D size batteries. These motors are available from most barbecue shops. The food is held in place on the spit rod by a couple of rotisserie prongs which are also available from barbecue stores.

There are a number of Australian made portable spit roasting units available, two being the Auspit and the Aussie Porta Spit. Both of these units come complete with spit bar, rotisserie motor, meat skewers/prongs and stand.

heat source

For spit roasting, a good, consistent heat source is required. The two main heat sources are coals and head beads or briquettes. Both need to be started in plenty of time prior to cooking

If using coals allow at least 1-2 hours to get a good supply of coals from your fire. It is also a good idea to have a small cooking fire nearby so you will have a constant supply of hot coals. This is important when roasting lamb or beef which have cooking times of a couple of hours.

If possible try to avoid positioning your cooking spit where it will be affected by the wind. Wind will add considerably to the cooking time so if it is windy rig up some form of windbreak.

For a different flavour to your meat, you can add 'flavoured' wood chips to your heat source. These wood chips can be purchased through barbecue and outdoor retailers.

securing food

When spit roasting it is important to ensure that the food is well secured to the spit rod. Skewer the meat with the spit rod, then secure it with the meat prongs and tighten these to the spit rod. If the meat is loose and moves around the rod, or there are pieces of meat hanging, use butcher's string to further secure the meat.

Food must be well balanced on the spit rod to ensure even cooking and to prevent alternating speeds from the motor. When using cuts of meat with a bone, such as a leg of lamb etc, push the spit rod through the meat directly next to the bone on the meatiest side, to give good balance.

To check if the food is well balanced, place tip of spit rod on the ground and spin to see if there is any roll over.

Once the food is ready to be cooked, place the spit rod about 15-20 centimetres above the heat for the first 15 minutes or so to sear the outside and seal in the juices. After this move the rod to a higher setting and cook until the juices flow clear.

cooking times

Cooking times will vary depending on the weight and type of food being cooked and how you prefer your meat cooked. The quality of the heat source and weather conditions will also effect the cooking times.

Use the times below as a guide only:

- Chicken 1-1½ hours
- Lamb 45 minutes per 500 g
- Beef 45 - 50 minutes per 500 g
- Pork 45 - 55 minutes per 500 g

spit roast chicken

spit roasting chicken

 Cooking time: around 1½ hours

SERVES 4

1 large chicken
Little butter or margarine
Salt and pepper to taste

When spit roasting chicken tie the legs together securely with string and tie string around the parson's nose so that legs and back are neatly shaped to the bird. Place a knob of butter and a sprig of parsley in the body cavity. If stuffing, fill loosely into the chicken and truss. Secure wings and flap over body cavity, to enclose stuffing, with a skewer.Secure the chicken to the spit rod and place over heat source. Whilst cooking brush chicken with melted butter and sprinkle with salt or seasoning of choice. Or use one of the suggested glazes or rubs.

Tip ~ Chicken can become dry during spit roasting, securing strips of bacon over the breast can help alleviate this (and the resulting cooked bacon is devine!).

spit roast beef, lamb & pork

Cooking time: around 45 minutes per 500 g

Piece of meat:
Beef - try silverside
Lamb - leg with bone, boned leg or shoulder
Pork - leg or rolled loin

Insert spit rod through centre of the meat, if using a piece with a bone, insert through meat beside the bone. Meats can be glazed or marinated, or make some slits in the meat and insert slivers of garlic and your favourite herb, or just enjoy the delightful smokey flavour of spit roasting. If roasting pork, first score the skin, then pour on some cooking oil and rub in a good quantity of salt. This will give you superb crackling. Spit roast meat over heat source until the meat is cooked to your liking.

spit roast beef & red wine

 Cooking time: around 2½ - 3 hours

SERVES 4-6

2 kg piece of beef
¼ cup melted butter
½ cup red wine
Ground black pepper
Salt

Insert spit rod through centre of the piece of beef and secure with prongs. Place over heat source and spit roast until cooked as desired. Combine melted butter, wine, good amount of black pepper and salt. Baste beef regularly with marinade during cooking.

greek style spit roast lamb

Cooking time: around 2½ - 3 hours

SERVES 6

2 kg leg of lamb
2 lemons, halved
1 teaspoon dried oregano
¼ cup olive oil
Salt and pepper

Thoroughly rub lemon over meat, squeezing juice and pulp into meat. Then rub oregano over meat. Let meat marinate in fridge overnight if possible. Insert spit rod through centre of the lamb leg along the bone and secure with prongs. Season with salt and pepper. Cook over heat source, regularly brushing with oil, until cooked as desired.

greek style spit roast lamb

spit roast pork loin

spit roast pork loin

 Cooking time: around 2½ - 3 hours

SERVES 4

2 kg rolled pork loin
2 cloves garlic
2 teaspoons of rosemary
2 teaspoons olive oil
Salt and pepper
1½ cups red wine

Cut one garlic clove into slivers. Cut slits all over pork and insert slivers of garlic along with some rosemary leaves. Crush the second garlic clove and combine with the balance of rosemary, salt, pepper and the oil. Rub this mixture all over the pork. Let marinate in the fridge for at least 2 to 3 hours. Remove meat from fridge at least 30 minutes prior to cooking and secure onto spit rod with prongs. Cook over heat source, brushing with the red wine every 20 minutes, until meat is cooked as desired.

fiery spit roast chicken

Cooking time: around 1½ hours

SERVES 4

1 large chicken

MARINADE
½ cup olive oil
¼ cup lemon juice
¼ cup orange juice
¼ cup red wine vinegar
2-3 tablespoons of Tabasco sauce or Piri-Piri sauce
2 teaspoons paprika
½ teaspoon ground cumin
4 garlic cloves, crushed
2 teaspoons of ginger
2 teaspoons thyme, fresh is best
1 tablespoon parsley, fresh is best
Salt and pepper to taste

Rinse the chicken and pat dry with paper towel and tie legs and parson's nose. In large bowl combine all marinade ingredients and mix well. Reserve about a ¼ cup of the marinade. Place chicken in bowl and turn to coat with marinade. Cover and refrigerate for at least 2 hours, turning chicken a few times. Remove from fridge 30 minutes prior to cooking. Secure chicken on spit rod and place over heat source. Spit roast for about 1½ hours or until juices run clear. Baste regularly with reserved marinade during cooking.

additional flavours

For some added flavour to your spit roast meat, try out one of these easy to make dry rubs or glazes or purchase ready made rubs and glazes from the supermarket. These can also be used for your camp oven roast or even for your barbecue meat.

all purpose dry rub

1 tablespoon dried basil
1 tablespoon dried thyme
1 tablespoon dried oregano
2 teaspoons dried rosemary
1 teaspoon salt
½ teaspoon ground pepper

Mix all ingredients together. Brush meat all over with oil. Rub the dry rub all over meat thoroughly. This rub works well for beef, lamb, pork and chicken.

lamb dry rub

1 tablespoon dried marjoram
1 tablespoon dried thyme
2 teaspoons dried oregano
2 teaspoons dried rosemary
1 teaspoon dried sage
½ teaspoon crushed fennel seeds
½ teaspoon salt
½ teaspoon ground pepper

Mix all ingredients together. Brush meat all over with oil. Rub the dry rub vigorously all over meat.

chicken dry rub

1 tablespoon chilli powder
1 tablespoon ground cumin
2 teaspoons dried oregano
2 teaspoons garlic powder
1 teaspoon onion powder
1 teaspoon dry mustard
1 teaspoon sweet paprika
1 teaspoon salt
½ teaspoon ground cayenne pepper

Mix all ingredients together. Brush chicken all over with oil. Rub the dry rub all over chicken thoroughly.

pork dry rub

2 teaspoons dried thyme
2 teaspoons ground allspice
1 teaspoon onion powder
1 teaspoon sugar
½ teaspoon grated nutmeg
½ teaspoon curry powder
½ teaspoon salt
¼ teaspoon ground cinnamon
¼ teaspoon cayenne pepper
Pinch ground cloves

Mix all ingredients together. Brush meat all over with oil. Rub the dry rub vigorously all over meat.

ginger honey glaze
for chicken

½ cup soy sauce
⅓ cup honey
2 teaspoons ground ginger

Mix ingredients and heat in small saucepan. Brush over chicken while on the spit.

orange honey glaze
for chicken

1 cup orange juice
¾ cup honey
1 teaspoon Worcestershire sauce

Mix ingredients and heat in small saucepan. Brush over chicken while on the spit.

bush camp, outback queensland

smoking

Smoking is a cooking method that seems to be increasing in popularity, even more so now with the number of portable smoke ovens on the market.

These ovens generally use the 'hot' smoking process where the food is placed in the smoking chamber on racks. A layer of sawdust is placed in the bottom of the oven and heat, usually from a spirit burner, is applied to the base of the oven, causing the sawdust to smoke. Just be sure the sawdust you use for smoking is free of contaminates. The best bet is to use sawdust that is especially packaged for smoking.

You can also use your camp oven to smoke food. Just use the same process as outlined above. However, place your camp oven over the fire instead of a spirit burner.

When smoking, the ovens produce high temperatures, so ensure that the oven is placed on a solid, heat resistant surface. And always use gloves to open the oven.

what to smoke?

Many different types of food can be smoked including sausages, chicken, eggs, beef, lamb and even nuts, with fish and prawns probably the most popular. The following recipes will give you an insight into cooking with a smoke oven. Most smoke ovens come with a recipe and hints book.

There are some suggestions that foods such as fish and chicken should be soaked in a brine mixture to help keep their moisture, however it is very much a personal preference. If you do wish to use the brine method, a good basic brine mixture can be made from 500 millilitres of water with 3 tablespoons of salt and 1-2 tablespoons of brown sugar. Soak the food for 15 minutes, take out and pat dry with paper towel, then smoke.

smoking times

As a rough guide foods such as fish, king prawns and most other seafood takes around 15 minutes to smoke. Chicken legs, sausages and smaller meat cuts require about 25-30 minutes cooking. A cup of methylated spirits will burn for 25-30 minutes.

smoked chicken breasts

chicken legs or wings

 Cooking time: 20-25 minutes

Legs or wings per person
1 cup of wine (red or white)
1 tablespoon honey
1 tablespoon soy sauce
1 garlic, clove crushed (optional)

Place all ingredients in a bowl and leave to marinate for at least an hour. Sprinkle 2 tablespoons of sawdust in smoker. Place chicken pieces on rack in smoker and smoke until cooked, about 20 minutes.

smoked chicken breasts

 Cooking time: around 20 minutes

Chicken breasts

Sprinkle 2 tablespoons of sawdust in smoker. Place chicken breasts on rack and smoke for 20 minutes. These smoked breasts are great sliced in a salad or used in a cream and seeded mustard sauce (fry diced onion and garlic in a little oil, add some cream or evaporated milk to pan with a tablespoon of seeded mustard, simmer over low heat, add sliced smoked chicken breast and heat through, great over pasta).

smoked prawns

 Cooking time: around 15-20 minutes

Green prawns, peeled and deveined
Wooden skewers, to fit smoker
Marinade or sauce of choice

Thread prawns onto wooden skewers. Place prawn skewers in shallow dish and cover with sauce and marinate until ready to cook. Sprinkle 2 tablespoons of sawdust in smoker. Place skewers on rack in smoker and smoke for 15 minutes.

smoked trout

 Cooking time: around 15-20 minutes

Gutted trout
Melted butter
Dried mixed herbs
Squeeze of lemon juice

Combine melted butter, mixed herbs and lemon juice. Brush inside of trout with the mixture. Sprinkle 2 tablespoons of sawdust in smoker. Place trout on rack in smoker and smoke for 20 minutes until tender.

smoked trout

smoked ribs

smoked ribs

 Cooking time: around 20-25 minutes

Pork spare ribs

Sprinkle 2 tablespoons of sawdust in smoker. Brush ribs with sauce, such as a smokey barbecue sauce or sweet and sour sauce, leave to marinate until ready to cook. Place pork ribs on rack and smoke for 20-30 minutes.

smoked lamb or pork chops

Cooking time: around 20-25 minutes

Lamb or pork chops of choice
Herb or spice of choice: eg: rosemary, steak spice or one of the widely available Grill & BBQ seasonings would be ideal

Rub both sides of chops with seasoning of choice. Sprinkle 2 tablespoons of sawdust in smoker. Place on rack in smoker and smoke for 20 minutes until cooked through.

Tip ~ This could also be done with chicken breasts.

smoked eggs

 Cooking time: around 15 minutes

Boiled eggs

Sprinkle 2 tablespoons of sawdust in smoker. Place shelled, boiled eggs on smoker rack. Smoke for 15 minutes until a pale golden colour. Enjoy these hot or cold, either by themselves seasoned with salt and pepper, on sandwiches, as part of a ploughman's lunch or an antipasto platter.

smoked snags

Cooking time: around 20 minutes

Sausages

Sprinkle 2 tablespoons of sawdust in smoker. Place sausages on rack and smoke for approximately 20 minutes.

*Tip ~ **This is a great way of cooking spicy sausages.***

ham steaks & pineapple

Want a twist to your ham steaks and pineapple? Smoke them instead of barbecuing.

 Cooking time: around 10-15 minutes

Ham steaks
Pineapple rings

Sprinkle 2 tablespoon of sawdust in smoker. Place ham steaks and pineapple rings on rack. Smoke for 10-15 minutes.

smoked snags & eggs

salads &
vegetables

These tasty salad and vegetable recipes make the
perfect accompaniment to any meat, fish or poultry dish.
It really is easy being green.

new chums pasta salad

2-3 cups of hot cooked pasta
1 cup corn kernels
4 shallots, chopped
1 capsicum, chopped
½ cup oil
¼ cup lemon juice
Salt and black pepper

Combine oil, lemon juice and salt and pepper in a jar and mix well. While pasta is still hot pour over dressing. Allow to cool. Once cooled, add vegetables and toss well.

Tip ~ Use ½ a cup of your favourite salad dressing instead.

curried pasta salad

SERVES **4**

2 cups of cooked pasta
1 capsicum, chopped
4 shallots, chopped
1 cup celery, sliced
1 cup mushrooms, sliced

CURRY DRESSING
2 tablespoons brown sugar
2 tablespoons curry powder
½ cup oil
½ cup white vinegar

Combine pasta and vegetables in bowl and mix well. Curry dressing, combine all ingredients in a smallscrew top jar and shake to mix well. Pour dressing over salad.

Tip ~ A tablespoon of cream can be added to the curry dressing.

rice salad

SERVES **4**

2-3 cups cooked rice
1 capsicum, chopped
4 shallots, chopped
310 g can corn kernels, drained
450 g can pineapple pieces, drained
⅓ cup sultanas
Salt and pepper to season

DRESSING
⅓ cup oil
2 tablespoons lemon juice
¼ teaspoon dry mustard
¼ teaspoon sugar

Combine rice with vegetables and fruit. Season with salt and pepper. Dressing, mix all ingredients in small screw top jar and shake well to mix. Pour dressing over salad and toss well.

Tip ~ Use 1 cup of store bought French Salad Dressing as an alternative.

fossickers hot onion salad

Cooking time: around 3-5 minutes
SERVES **4**

3-4 medium sized onions, sliced
⅓ cup oil
½ cup red wine
1 tablespoon seeded mustard
2 teaspoons honey
1 teaspoon dried mixed herbs

Combine all ingredients in a bowl and leave to marinate (the longer the better). Cook on barbecue plate until onions are soft. Delicious served with barbecued meat.

char grilled vegies

char grilled vegies

Sliced vegetables such as zucchini, eggplant, potato, sweet potato, pumpkin, squash and asparagus can all be char grilled over hot coals. Potato, sweet potato and pumpkin should be parboiled first until just tender. Place vegetables on well oiled grill over hot coals. Brush vegetables with oil and grill until tender.

Tip ~ Sprinkle with your favourite seasoning while cooking

pesto potato salad

SERVES 4

3 large potatoes, peeled and cubed
½ cup mayonnaise
1 tablespoon bottled pesto

Boil potatoes until just tender. Whilst boiling, mix mayonnaise and pesto together. Stir mayonnaise mixture through cooked potatoes until well covered.

corn salad

SERVES 4

420 g tin of corn, drained
1 red capsicum, sliced
1 green capsicum, sliced

DRESSING
⅓ cup mayonnaise
1 tablespoon lemon juice
½ teaspoon ground cumin

Combine corn and capsicum. For the dressing, combine all ingredients in a screw top jar and shake well to combine. Pour dressing over corn and capsicum.

bean salad

SERVES 4

430 g can 3 Bean Mix, drained and rinsed
1 onion, sliced
1 capsicum, sliced
2 tomatoes, diced

Mix all vegetables together then pour over your favourite salad dressing.

couscous salad

SERVES **4**

1½ cups couscous
1½ cups boiling water
⅓ cup dried currants
2 teaspoons grated lemon rind
2 teaspoons lemon juice
¼ cup coriander leaves, chopped

Place couscous and boiling water in boil. Let stand for 5 minutes until water is absorbed. Fluff couscous with a fork. Add remaining ingredients and mix well to combine. This is great served with tandoori lamb cutlets, see page 39.

vegie patties

Potato, Carrot, Zucchini
Egg
Salt and pepper
Flour

Grate all vegetables. Add egg, seasoning and enough flour to vegetables to make a thick batter. Spoon vegetable batter onto hot oiled barbecue plate. Cook until brown, turn over and cook other side. Delicious served as a snack or as a side dish to barbecue meat.

*Tip ~ **Use whatever vegetables you may have.***

thai salad base

Mixed salad leaves
Red onion, thinly sliced
Cherry tomatoes, halved
Lebanese cucumber, thinly sliced
Coriander leaves – optional
Chilli & Lime dressing – or similar

Combine all salad ingredients in a bowl or on a serving platter. Drizzle with dressing.

*Tip ~ **This is an easy salad base to which some thinly sliced barbecued or stir fried beef or chicken, which have been brushed with a chilli sauce or paste, can be added. Or slice up some smoked chicken breast from page 147. Shredded cabbage can replace the salad leaves.***

couscous salad

gado gado salad

2 carrots, thinly sliced
Handful of sliced green beans
1 cup shredded cabbage
1 cucumber, thinly sliced
2 hard boiled eggs
2 spring onions sliced
Bottled satay sauce

Place carrots and beans in a pot of boiling water for 2 minutes. Drain and refresh with cold water. Arrange all vegetables on a serving platter with sliced boiled eggs. Drizzle satay sauce over vegetables.

Tip ~ This is a nice easy salad that looks pretty impressive, and is a great way to use up vegetables. Bean sprouts can also be added.

vegetable kebabs

Cooking time: around 5-10 minutes

Onion wedges
Capsicums
Button mushrooms
Cherry tomatoes or tomato wedges
Eggplant
Zucchini
Pineapple cubes

MARINADE
1 tablespoon oil
1 tablespoon soy source
1 tablespoon pineapple juice

Cut larger vegetables such as eggplant and zucchini into bite sized cubes. Thread vegetables and fruit on skewers. Cook on lightly oiled barbecue plate or grill brushing with marinade until vegetables are heated through and tender.

Tip ~ Any mix of vegetables can be used.

vegetable kebabs

pan fried potatoes & bacon

pan fried potatoes & bacon

 Cooking time: around 15 minutes

SERVES 4

3 medium sized potatoes, peeled, diced and boiled
until just tender
1 tablespoon plain flour
2 shallots, chopped
¼ cup cream
2 bacon rashers, finely chopped

Place drained potatoes in a bowl. Combine flour, shallots and cream. Mix cream mixture with potatoes. Cook bacon until crispy in frying pan. Pour potato mixture on top of bacon and cook until potato mixture browns on the bottom. Turn mixture over and brown other side.

Tip ~ This tasty recipe is ideal to use up left over boiled potatoes.

cheesey potatoes

Cooking time: around 50 minutes

SERVES 4

4 large potatoes, peeled
Pinch of paprika
Pinch of garlic salt
4-5 cheese slices
1 tablespoon melted butter

Cut potatoes in half and place, cut side down, in greased camp oven or greased dish. Sprinkle with pinch of paprika and garlic salt. Bake in moderate coals until potatoes are tender, approximately 40 minutes. Cover potatoes with cheese slices, brush with melted butter. Cook in coals with coals on lid until cheese has melted, approximately 7-10 minutes.

Tip ~ For a change place strips of bacon, ham, smoked salmon, onion or tomato on the potatoes before placing the cheese on top.

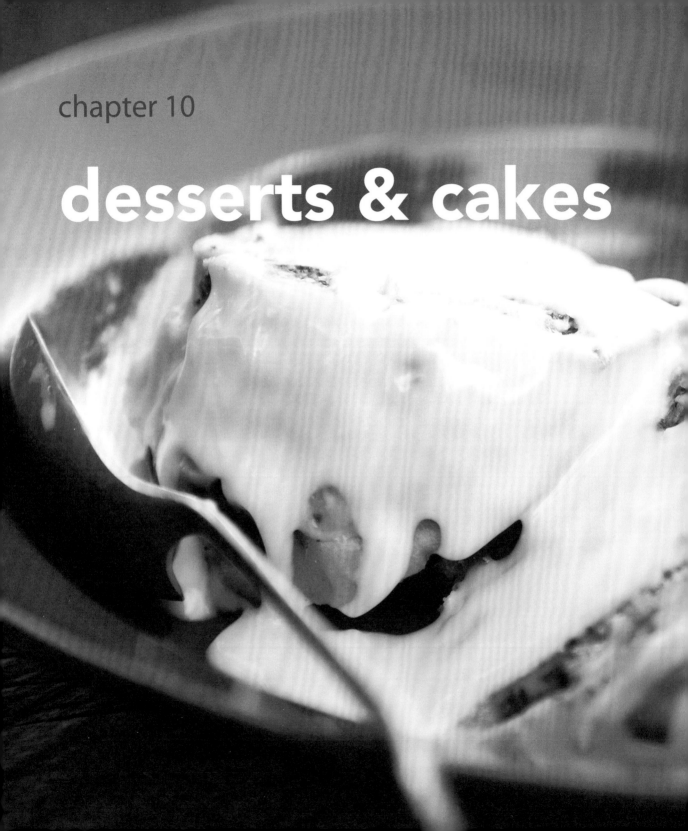

desserts & cakes

An evening meal in the outdoors without a tempting
dessert to finish is like a meat pie without sauce
—they just go together! Try a few of these recipes and
you'll know what we mean.

creamy coconut bananas

 Cooking time: around 5 minutes

SERVES 4

3–4 bananas, peeled and sliced
2 tablespoons honey
1 cup coconut milk
Vanilla essence

Warm coconut milk, honey and a sprinkle of vanilla in a saucepan. Stir until the honey has dissolved. Add sliced bananas. Bring to the boil and stir for about 1 minute. Serve hot or cold.

outback bananas

Cooking time: around 15 minutes

Bananas – one or two per person
Foil squares to fit bananas

FILLING IDEAS
Chocolate buds and marshmallows
Honey and cinnamon sugar
Chopped up chocolate bars such as Mars bar or Bounty bar

Place peeled bananas on the foil square and slice lengthways down the middle of banana. Do not cut the whole way through. Place filling down the cut in the banana. Wrap foil around the banana tightly and place on grill over hot coals. Slowly cook bananas turning over once or twice until they are heated through and soft. Carefully open foil and slide bananas into bowl.

Tip ~ For those who like to ramp up the calories at dessert, serve with custard and/or cream.

outback bananas

rice pudding with
rummy fruits

no bake biccies

ginger cream log

boiling spotted dog

rice pudding

 Cooking time: around 2 hours

SERVES 4

½ cup medium or short grain rice
1 tablespoon soft brown sugar
2 tablespoons sultanas
1 teaspoon grated orange rind
3 cups milk
½ teaspoon ground cinnamon
2 teaspoons soft brown sugar

Use a 4-cup capacity dish that fits in camp oven. Brush dish with melted butter. Place rice in dish. Sprinkle sugar, sultanas and orange rind over rice. Pour milk over the rice. Place dish in heated camp oven and bake in slow coals for 1¾ hours. Combine cinnamon and sugar. Sprinkle over pudding and bake for a further 20 minutes until pudding is firm.

rummy fruits

Cooking time: 10-15 minutes

SERVES 4

12 dried apricots
12 dried prunes
½ cup raisins or sultanas
1 cup orange juice
1 cinnamon stick
4 bananas, peeled and thickly sliced
1-2 tablespoons of rum

Place apricots, prunes, raisins, orange juice and cinnamon stick in pan. Bring to boil and simmer for 10 minutes. Add bananas and simmer for a further 2 minutes. Add rum and stir through. Serve with custard, creamed rice or rice pudding.

lemon banana pancakes

 Cooking time: 5-10 minutes
SERVES 4-6

10 large basic pancakes
½ cup mashed banana
½ cup thickened cream
1 tablespoon lemon juice
1 tablespoon caster sugar

Prepare pancakes (see basic pancake mix on page 26) and keep warm wrapped in foil to side of fire. Mix banana, cream, lemon juice and sugar together. Spread mixture liberally on pancakes. Roll up and sprinkle with a little extra caster sugar.

cocky's joy dumplings

Cooking time: 30 minutes
SERVES 6-8

DUMPLINGS
2 cups self-raising flour
1 tablespoon sugar
Pinch salt
1 tablespoon butter
1 egg
Enough milk to make a soft dough
Extra flour

SYRUP
3 cups water
3 tablespoons golden syrup
2 tablespoons sugar
1 tablespoon butter

SYRUP: Put all syrup ingredients into camp oven or large saucepan and bring to the boil.
DUMPLINGS: Rub butter into flour until it resembles bread crumbs. Add egg and enough milk to make dough. Roll dough into small balls and lightly cover with extra flour. Drop dumplings into boiling syrup. Cover and boil dumplings in syrup for 20 minutes. Serve dumplings with syrup poured over and custard or cream.

Tip ~ Instead of boiling, these dumplings can be baked. Place dumplings in a dish or directly into camp oven, pour syrup mixture over and bake in moderate coals for 20 minutes.

cocky's joy dumplings

spotted dog

spotted dog

This boiled pudding requires a bit of effort with the pre planning, but the effort is well worth it – this is what old-style bush puddings are all about. As they say, the proof is in the pudding!

Cooking time: around 3 hours
SERVES 6-8

2 cups self-raising flour
¼ cup sugar
½ teaspoon nutmeg
250 g currants
2 teaspoons butter
Clean cloth – piece of calico, tea towel
or even a ham bag

Place a trivet or pie dish in base of the camp oven – to stop pudding hitting the bottom. Then fill with water and get on the boil. Dissolve the butter in 300 ml of hot water. Mix the flour, sugar, nutmeg and currants in a large bowl. Then add the hot water and butter mixture. Mix together and add extra hot water to make a sloppy mixture. When mixed, pour into the clean cloth and pull sides up and tie with butchers twine. Tie the cloth up just above the mixture leaving a little room for it to expand. Place pudding in the boiling water in the camp oven, cover and boil for 3 hours. Ensure that the pudding mix is constantly covered with water. Keep a billy or two filled with boiling water so as extra water can be added to the camp oven as necessary. After 3 hours remove the cloth and open the pudding. Place on a dish and let it cool slightly. Serve hot with custard.

Tip ~ When the pudding is taken directly out of the water, you will notice that the outside of the pudding is soft and looks uncooked – don't worry, it's cooked.

bread 'n butter pudding

 Cooking time: around 45-50 minutes

SERVES 4-6

8-10 slices of stale bread
4 eggs
2 cups milk
¼ cup jam of choice or sugar
Butter
1 teaspoon vanilla essence, optional
3 tablespoons sultanas or chopped dried apricots,
optional
Nutmeg to taste

Remove crusts from bread and spread one side with butter and jam or sugar. Cut into fingers or squares. Place a layer of bread, butter and jam side up, in a lightly buttered tin or dish or straight into the camp oven. Sprinkle with sultanas or apricots if using. Place second layer of bread, butter and jam side down on top of first layer. Beat eggs, sugar, milk and vanilla together. Pour egg mixture over bread and let stand for 15 minutes while the bread absorbs all liquid. Sprinkle with some nutmeg. Bake in camp oven with medium coals on base and on lid for 45 minutes or until the top is browned.

Tip ~ This is a great way of using up that stale bread!

apple crumble

Cooking time: around 30 minutes

SERVES 4-6

800 g can tinned apple
1 cup self-raising flour
½ cup brown sugar
½ teaspoon cinnamon
½ cup butter

Mix together flour, sugar, cinnamon and butter until it resembles bread crumbs. Place apples in pie dish and cover with flour mixture. Bake in camp oven with medium coals on bottom and hotter coals on top, for 25-30 minutes until top is golden.

Tip ~ For a different taste sprinkle a handful of sultanas over the apples or use peaches sprinkled with some crushed cloves. Porridge oats can be added to the crumble mixture.

apple crumble

dungaree settlers baked apples

dungaree settlers baked apples

Cooking time: around 30-40 minutes

SERVES 6

6 large green cooking apples
2 tablespoons of chopped dates
2 tablespoons of sultanas
1 teaspoon cinnamon
½ teaspoon ground cloves
Brown sugar
Butter

Core apples. Slice through the peel around the apple about halfway down a couple of times. This will stop the apples from bursting. Mix together dates, sultanas, cinnamon and ground cloves. Fill apple centres with date mixture. Sprinkle top of apples with brown sugar and dot with butter. Bake on tray or foil in camp oven, over medium coals, until apples are soft. Around 30 minutes depending on coals. Serve with custard and cream.

rockleigh apples

Cooking time: around 15-20 minutes

SERVES 4

4 apples, peeled, cored and sliced
1 cup orange juice
3 tablespoons raw sugar
1 teaspoon cinnamon
Port, optional

Cook apples in orange juice, sugar and cinnamon and port (if using) until just tender. Serve apples with warm liquid and custard or cream. This is a great no fuss dessert.

murrah pudding

 Cooking time: around 5 minutes

SERVES 4

1-2 slices stale white bread per person
½ cup milk
1 teaspoon white sugar
1 egg yolk, lightly beaten
Butter for frying
Jam of choice, heated

Cut crusts from bread. Combine milk and sugar. Dip bread into milk mixture. Drain bread then dip into egg yolk. Heat butter in frying pan or on barbecue plate. Fry bread on both sides until golden brown. Serve with hot jam poured over each slice.

Tip ~ Keep the egg white and use in scrambled eggs the next morning.

paroo peach pie

 Cooking time: around 20-30 minutes

SERVES 4-6

825 g can sliced peaches, drained
2 tablespoons butter
½ cup sugar (caster if you have some)
1 teaspoon vanilla essence
1 egg
1 cup self-raising flour
½ cup milk
¼ desiccated coconut

Arrange peaches over base of a pie dish. Cream butter, sugar and vanilla together and gradually beat in the egg. Add dry ingredients and milk. Mix until smooth. Spread butter mixture over the peaches and sprinkle with extra coconut. Bake in camp oven until golden and top is set. Serve hot with custard.

paroo peach pie

silver city lemon pudding

silver city lemon pudding

 Cooking time: around 30-35 minutes

SERVES 4

¾ cup self-raising flour
3 tablespoons butter, softened
¾ cup caster sugar
2 eggs
Grated rind of 1 lemon
1-2 tablespoons milk

SAUCE
¾ cup caster sugar
2 tablespoons cornflour
Juice of 1 lemon
Boiling water

Grease a pie dish that fits into camp oven. In a large bowl beat together flour, butter, sugar, eggs and lemon rind. Best to use a wooden spoon for this. Gradually add milk to make a smooth consistency. Spread mixture into pie dish. SAUCE: Combine (carefully!) lemon juice and boiling water to make 1¼ cup of liquid. Mix together the sugar and cornflour. Gradually add the lemon juice mixture to the cornflour and mix well. Pour sauce over the top. Bake in camp oven on trivet over hot coals for 30-35 minutes or when the mixture is golden and firm on top.

fruity kebabs

Cooking time: around 10-15 minutes

SERVES 4

Fruit of choice, either fresh or tinned such as: pineapple, apple, mango, kiwi fruit, peach, banana, etc
2 tablespoons honey
Juice of 1 lemon
2 tablespoons of favourite spirit: such as brandy, rum or mailbu - optional
Jam of choice, heated

Combine honey, lemon juice and spirit if using. Maybe a good idea to leave the spirit out if cooking these for the kids! Cook kebabs on lightly oiled grill or hot plate, brushing with marinade until nicely warmed through.

jam roly-poly

 Cooking time: around 30-40 minutes

SERVES 4-6

2 cups self-raising flour
Pinch salt
3 tablespoons butter
Water
¾ cup jam, apricot is delicious
½ cup sultanas, optional
1 teaspoon melted butter

Mix flour and salt together in a bowl and rub in butter. Slowly add enough water to make a dough. On lightly floured surface, roll dough out into a thin rectangle. Spread jam on dough lengthways, if using sultanas sprinkle over jam. Roll dough up lengthways. Place dough-roll into a greased pie dish, loaf tin or plate. Using a sharp knife make a few slits in the top of roll and lightly spread with melted butter. Bake in camp oven with medium coals on bottom and hot coals on top for about 30 to 40 minutes. Serve hot with custard or whipped cream.

lattice slice

SERVES 4
MAKES 8-10 SQUARES

1 packet of Lattice biscuits
1 packet of White Wings Vanilla pudding mix
½ cup milk
½ cup cream

Line a container with baking paper, with extra hanging out the ends. Using half of the lattice biscuits place a layer in the container.
Beat the pudding mix, milk and cream together until it thickens and is smooth. Pour pudding mix over the biscuits and then place a second layer of biscuits on top. Chill before cutting between the biscuits.

Tip ~ For a change from the vanilla pudding mix – try the chocolate pudding mix.

lattice slice

caramel pie

caramel pie

 Cooking time: around 15 minute

SERVES 4-6

Quantity of shortcrust pastry, adding sugar to mix
as noted in the Tip - see page 212
380 g tin of Nestle Top'n'Fill Caramel
Rice for pastry cooking

Line base and sides of pie dish or flan tin with the
shortcrust pastry. Prick the base of the pastry with
a fork and then line with some baking paper and
pour in some rice to cover the base. Bake on a trivet
in heated camp oven over moderately hot coals for
10 minutes. Remove the rice and the baking paper
and return the pie dish to camp oven and bake for a
further 5 minutes until pastry has lightly browned.
Once pastry has cooled spoon the caramel filling in
and place in fridge to set and cool.

Tip ~ Thickly sliced bananas can be placed on the
pastry shell before spooning in the caramel.

ginger cream log

SERVES 4-6

250 g packet Ginger Nut biscuits
400 g can crushed pineapple drained,
juice reserved
300 ml carton cream, whipped
1 tablespoon brandy or rum, optional

Mix pineapple with half the whipped cream.
Place the biscuits in a log shape on a large
piece of foil. Spread the cream and pineapple
mixture on and between the biscuits, pressing them
against each other and keeping the biscuits in a
log shape. Sprinkle with 1 tablespoon of reserved
juice and your choice of spirit. Roll the foil up
tightly around the log and chill overnight. To serve
place the log on a serving plate and cover with the
remaining whipped cream.

Tip ~ This dessert log is delicious. The only real
effort to make this is whipping the cream — if
you have the patience to do this by hand whilst at
camp you will definitely enjoy this dessert or enjoy
it with an afternoon coffee.

simple pineapple cake

 Cooking time: around 1 hour

SERVES **6-8**

2 cups self raising flour
1 cup sugar
440 g tin of crushed pineapple

Combine flour and sugar in large bowl. Add the crushed pineapple. Mix well. At this point I sometimes add a lid full of rum. Pour mixture into a well greased and floured cake tin. Place cake tin on trivet in camp oven and bake in moderate to hot camp oven with coals around base and on lid for 1 hour until cake is cooked through. Use a clean skewer to check that the centre is cooked through.

shearers smoko cake

Cooking time: around 1-1½ hours

SERVES **6-8**

2 cups dried mixed fruit
1¼ cups brown sugar
1 cup strong black tea
1 egg, lightly beaten
4 tablespoons golden syrup
4 cups self-raising flour
1 teaspoon mixed spice: cinnamon, nutmeg, cloves

Place fruit and brown sugar in bowl and pour tea over. Cover and let stand overnight. Grease cake tin and/or line with baking paper if you have it. Combine egg, golden syrup, flour and spice to the fruit and tea. Mix well. Spoon mixture into prepared cake tin and place on trivet inside camp oven. Bake in camp oven for 1 to 1½ hours with medium hot coals on the base and on lid.

Tip ~ This is a really heavy cake batter and is best baked in a larger sized cake tin that's not too high and left to cool for 4 hours before cutting.

shearers smoko cake

rum balls & lemon slice

the easiest rum balls

MAKES ABOUT 40 BALLS

8 weet-bix, crushed
1 cup sweetened condensed milk
2 tablespoons cocoa or drinking chocolate
1 cup chopped dried fruit, try dates, apricots or prunes
¼ cup rum
1 cup desiccated coconut
Extra coconut

Combine all ingredients and mix well. Place in fridge for 10-15 minutes. Roll into small balls and then cover with extra desiccated coconut.

*Tip ~ **Keep stored in the fridge. These get better after a couple of days! Serve up with a port after a great bush camp meal or even with a cuppa for afternoon tea.***

no bake lemon slice

SERVES 10-12

250 g packet of Ginger Nut or Milk Arrowroot biscuits, crushed
⅔ cup sweetened condensed milk
1 cup desiccated coconut
4 tablespoons butter, melted
Grated rind of 2 lemons

LEMON ICING
1½ cups icing sugar
1 teaspoon butter
2 tablespoon lemon juice – approximately

Mix together crushed biscuits and coconut. Add condensed milk, butter and lemon rind. Mix well. Press mixture into greased slice/lamington tin and refrigerate for an hour or until set.
LEMON ICING
Place icing sugar in bowl and stir in softened butter. Mix in enough lemon juice to make the icing a spreadable consistency. Spread icing over slice. Cut into slices and enjoy with a cuppa.

*Tip ~ **This slice is best kept in the fridge.***

no bake biccies

MAKES ABOUT 60 BICCIES

2 cups white sugar
⅓ cup cocoa powder
½ cup milk
125 g butter
3 cups rolled oats
1½ cups shredded coconut
½ cup chopped walnuts

In large saucepan mix together sugar and cocoa powder. Add milk and butter. Over high heat add oats, coconut and walnuts. Mix well. Quickly drop rounded teaspoonfuls of mixture onto greaseproof paper. Allow 1 hour to set.

anzac biscuits

Cooking time: around 5-10 minutes
MAKES ABOUT 20 BISCUITS

1 cup rolled oats
1 cup desiccated coconut
1 cup plain flour
½ cup white sugar
125 g butter
1 tablespoon golden syrup
1 teaspoon bicarbonate of soda
3 tablespoons boiling water

In a large bowl mix well the rolled oats, coconut, flour and sugar. In small saucepan heat the butter and golden syrup. Dissolve the bicarbonate of soda in the boiling water, then add to the butter and golden syrup. Pour the liquid into the dry ingredients and mix well. Drop dessertspoon mounds onto a greased tray, place on trivet in hot camp oven and bake with moderate coals on the base and lid until golden brown. Once these are golden brown they will still be slightly soft - allow them to cool on the tray for a few minutes then lift them off onto a trivet or cake cooler to cool down

Tip ~ Keep an eye on these as they can burn really quickly.

anzac biscuits

high country pikelets

high country pikelets

Cooking time: around 3-5 minutes
MAKES ABOUT 20

1 cup self raising flour
¼ cup castor sugar
¼ teaspoon bicarbonate of soda
1 egg
¾ cup milk
1 teaspoon white vinegar
½ tablespoon butter, melted

Combine flour, sugar and soda into a bowl. Make a well in the centre. Combine egg, milk and vinegar and mix until smooth. Gradually pour egg and milk mixture into the dry ingredients. Mix until smooth. Heat frying pan over heat and lightly grease with butter. Drop dessertspoons of batter into the pan, allowing room for spreading. When bubbles appear flip the pikelets and cook until golden brown on the other side.

Tip ~ The batter is best if it is left to stand for a while. If you do this, the batter will become thicker so you will need to add a little more milk to make the batter thinner and easier to pour. Another tip is to pour the batter from the tip of the spoon to get nice rounded pikelets – although I've never mastered the art of nice neat round pikelets or pancakes for that matter!

dried fruit salad

SERVES 4

500 g mixed dried fruits (apples, peaches, sultanas, apricots, etc)
1½ cups hot unsweetened black tea
Juice of 1 lemon
Honey or sugar to taste

Place dried fruit in a bowl and cover with fresh tea. Leave to stand for the day or overnight. Add lemon juice and honey or sugar to taste, mix well. Serve with custard for an easy dessert or yoghurt for a delicious breakfast.

Tip ~ This is best made in the morning so it can stand during the day for the fruit to swell to be ready for dessert that evening or alternatively make it in the evening and leave overnight to be ready for breakfast the following morning.

chapter 11

damper, bread, scones & muffins

During the early days of European settlement in Australia, bush travelers, stockmen and miners frequently survived on little more than tea and damper, with a little salted meat. The tea could have been made from tea-tree leaves or sassafras bark and the damper made of plain flour and water, and if supplies were available salt would have been added. The flour and water was mixed into a dough and shaped into a flat circle about six centimetres thick, then placed in a hole made in the hot ashes of the camp fire. More ashes were moved over the top to keep air out, to prevent the damper burning. After thirty minutes tiny cracks would appear on the surface from where steam had escaped. The damper was cooked if it sounded hollow when gently tapped with a stick.

In time a rising agent was added to the dough to make it lighter and more digestible. Camp ovens started to be used, protecting the damper from the ashes. Sometimes dripping or lard was used as was milk, sour milk or buttermilk as a substitute for water. Damper variations included Johnny-cakes (small dampers or scones), devil-on-the-coals (pieces of damper cooked quickly on the embers and turned by hand), sinkers (small balls of dough with fat mixed in and then boiled to make dumplings) and leather-jackets (scones fried in whatever fat was available).

damper

The traditional damper recipe is now often adapted by keen cooks, campers and bushwalkers: self raising flour is used to substitute the need for a rising agent, and oil or milk used instead of water.

damper or bread?

Many people's first thoughts when they purchase a camp oven is about baking mouth-watering dampers dripping with butter and lashings of golden syrup or cocky's joy. Sounds good doesn't it?

Generally, most people—us included, prefer bread to damper. With the advent of pre-packaged bread mixes and the wide availability of bread, even in the outback areas, the time honoured practice of making damper is fast becoming a dying art. We encourage you to help keep this bush staple alive and well!

beer damper

mixing beer damper

basic damper mix

 Cooking time: around 30-40 minutes

3 cup self-raising flour
1 cup milk or water
Pinch of salt

Mix ingredients together until all the flour has been incorporated. A knife can be used to do this. Shape dough and lightly dust with flour. Place into a greased camp oven and cover. Cook in medium coals, check after 30 minutes. Damper is cooked when it has a golden crust and a skewer inserted comes out clean

Variations to the basic damper recipe
Savoury: add onion, bacon, grated cheese, sliced olives, capsicum or mixed herbs.

Sweet: add honey, jam, sultanas, chocolate chips, nuts or sugar.

Dessert: shape dough into a long thick snake and twist it around a stick. Cook in the camp oven or loosely wrap some foil around it and cook in the coals. When cooked it comes away with a hollow centre. Fill the centre with jam or golden syrup and cream.

Cheese: when moulding the dough, place a wedge of camembert or brie cheese in the centre of the damper.

beer damper

Cooking time: around 30-40 minutes

4 cups self-raising flour
1 tablespoon butter or margarine
Can or stubby of beer – to get the best result use a beer with a yeast sediment in the bottom such as Coopers

Place flour in bowl. Make a well in the centre and add the butter and beer. Mix to a soft dough. Add extra flour if needed. Shape dough into a ball and slightly flatten. Place on greased tray in camp oven, cover and place over medium hot coals, adding coals to the lid. Bake until well risen and brown. Check after 30 minutes.

Tip ~ Don't have a camp oven? Trying cooking a damper in a billy with a lid.

pan-fried bread

If you don't have a camp oven you can make your own bread by using a heavy based frying pan — try this pan-fried bread.

 Cooking time: around 30 minutes

3 cups self-raising flour
2 tablespoons oil
1 cup warm water

Mix all ingredients and knead for a few minutes until dough is rubbery and elastic. Cover and leave for 30 minutes. Divide into small balls and pat flat. Fry bread in a frying pan or on hot plate in hot oil until golden. Drain on paper towels before serving.

easy bread

Making bread this traditional way with two risings can be time consuming but I love watching it rise and enjoy the punching and kneading process.

Cooking time: around 40 minutes

1 pre-packaged bread mix with yeast sachet

Combine bread flour with yeast sachet and add quantity of water as detailed on the package. Mix well. Knead dough on lightly floured board until smooth and sticky. Place dough in a bowl and cover with a tea towel. Leave for an hour until bread rises till about double its size. Take dough out of bowl and punch down, then knead again for about 10 minutes. Shape dough and place on lightly greased pan or in a greased loaf tin and leave in a warm spot till it doubles in size. Then place in heated camp oven and bake with coals all around the oven and on top, for approximately 40 minutes. Bread is cooked with a skewer comes out clean and sounds hollow when tapped.

easy bread

scones

scones

 Cooking time: around 10 minutes

MAKES APPROXIMATELY 16 SCONES

2 cups self-raising flour
2 teaspoons sugar
½ tablespoon butter
1 cup milk

Combine flour and sugar into bowl and rub butter in with fingers. Make a well in centre, and add nearly all the milk. Using a knife to cut the milk through the flour mixture, make a soft, sticky dough. Add remaining milk if needed. Roll dough out on a lightly floured surface and give a very quick knead. Press dough out to a 2 cm thickness. Cut dough into squares or use a cup to make rounds and place onto a greased baking tray. Brush a little milk on tops of scones. Place baking tray on trivet in hot camp oven and bake for 10 minutes or until tops are browned and scones sound hollow when tapped.

Tip ~ Folk lore suggests that the scones should be placed against each other on the baking tray. This supposedly helps the scones to rise better when baking.

drover's soda bread

Cooking time: around 40 minutes

3 cups wholemeal flour
1 cup plain white flour
1 teaspoon salt
1 teaspoon bicarbonate of soda
1 tablespoon butter
Approximately 500 ml of milk

Mix dry ingredients. Rub butter in with fingers. Make a well in the centre and gradually add milk, only add enough to make mixture soft, and mix until the dough is spongy. Turn dough onto floured surface and knead. Shape into a loaf about 5 cm thick. Place on lightly greased tray and brush the top with milk. Slash the top of the dough with a sharp knife about two or three times, this stops the crust cracking. Bake in camp oven on moderate coals with coals on lid for about 40 minutes. Check halfway through.

date scones

Cooking time: around 10-15 minutes

MAKES 12 SCONES

3 cups self-raising flour
1 tablespoon icing sugar
1 cup dates, chopped
1 egg, beaten
300 ml carton cream
300 ml lemonade
¼ teaspoon salt

Place flour and icing sugar in bowl, then add in the chopped dates and combine well. Add egg, cream and lemonade. Mix well. Roll dough out on a floured surface and knead quickly. Press dough out to a 2 cm thickness. Cut dough into squares or use a cup to make rounds and place onto a greased baking tray. Place baking tray on trivet in hot camp oven and bake for 10-15 minutes or until tops are browned.

Tip ~ If you don't have icing sugar replace with caster sugar. This is a very sticky dough so keep some flour at hand to use when kneading and rolling out. These scones are very light and tasty. We have trouble stopping at one, two ...

basic muffin mix

Cooking time: around 20-30 minutes

MAKES 6 LARGE MUFFINS OR 12 SMALL MUFFINS

2 cups self-raising flour
2 tablespoons soft brown sugar
1 egg
1 cup milk

Place flour and sugar in bowl, add egg and milk. Mix well. Spoon into greased muffin pan and bake in camp oven with medium coals for about 20-30 minutes. Check after 20 minutes. Muffins are cooked when a skewer comes out clean. Rest muffins in the pan for 5 minutes, then shake out.

Tip ~ I use wholemeal self-raising flour as it gives the muffins a great consistency. Grease muffin pan with butter and then sprinkle with a light dusting of flour.

Variations to the basic muffin mix
<u>Fruit:</u> add your favourite fruit – fresh or tinned: grated apple; mashed banana; grated pear; sultanas; berries.
<u>Savoury:</u> omit the brown sugar and add: herbs; cooked bacon; cooked onion; grated cheese.

blueberry muffins

cheese & herb muffins

cheese & herb muffins

 Cooking time: around 20 minutes
MAKES 10-12 MUFFINS

3 cups self-raising flour
½ cup full cream milk powder
Salt and pepper
2 tablespoons butter
1 teaspoon each of dried oregano, basil, parsley
1 cup grated tasty cheese
2 eggs, lightly beaten
1½ cups water

Place flour, milk powder, salt and pepper into bowl. Using your fingers rub in butter. Add dried herbs, cheese, eggs and water. Mix well. Spoon into greased muffin tin. Place muffin tin inside camp oven. Cover and place over medium to hot coals with coals on lid. Cook for 20 minutes. If not completely cooked, return to heat on base and lid and continue until muffins are well cooked and a skewer comes out clean when inserted.

yoghurt muffins

 Cooking time: around 30 minutes
MAKES 6 MUFFINS

2 cups self-raising flour
½ cup brown sugar
½ teaspoon cinnamon
1 egg, lightly beaten
½ cup milk
200 g Fruche yoghurt – with or without fruit
3 mashed bananas or stewed apples

Mix flour, sugar and cinnamon together. Add all other ingredients and mix up lightly. Spoon into large greased 6-cup muffin pan. Place muffin pan into camp oven and bake in moderate coals for approximately 30 minutes.

Tip ~ Half a cup of crushed walnuts or pecans can be added.

pizza dough

This will make enough dough for two 28 cm pizzas

7 g sachet dried yeast
½ teaspoon sugar
½ teaspoon salt
1 cup warm water
2½ cups plain flour

Combine yeast, sugar, salt and water in bowl. Cover with plastic wrap and stand in warm place until mixture is foamy, around 10 minutes. Place flour in large bowl and make a well in centre. Add the yeast mixture and mix to a dough. Knead dough on a floured surface until it becomes smooth and elastic, this should take 5 to 10 minutes. Roll out to desired size and thickness. Place on greased tray and top with favourite pizza toppings.

Tip ~ We like a nice firm pizza base so we usually bake the base for about 5-10 minutes prior to adding our toppings. Place the base on a tray and using a fork, prick the base a couple of times.

shortcrust pastry

This should make enough to use for base and lid of a 20 cm pie dish.

2 cups plain flour
½ teaspoon salt
½ cup milk or water
4 tablespoons butter, softened but not melted

Blend flour and salt together. Mix in butter with fingertips until mixture looks a bit like breadcrumbs. Slowly add milk or water and mix until there is no dry flour left and you have a stiff dough. Knead on floured board until smooth. Roll out to size.

Tip ~ For a sweet pastry add 1 tablespoon of sugar with flour and salt.

puff pastry

250 g plain flour
¾ cup butter, in small cubes
1 egg
6 tablespoons cold water
2 teaspoons lemon juice

Place flour in bowl and cut in butter. Mix egg, water and lemon juice together and stir into flour mixture until it forms a ball. Knead lightly on floured board and roll out. Fold one side of pastry into the middle, then fold the other side on top of it. Roll flat and make one quarter turn to the left. Repeat the folding, rolling and turning three times. Rest pastry in a cool place 30 minutes or more before use.

*Tip ~ **Ideal for pies, sausage rolls and quiches.***

emergency pie base

2 tablespoons butter
200g plain biscuits

Crush biscuits finely and mix in melted butter. Press firmly into base of pie dish. Refrigerate base until firm before using.

*Tip ~ **For a sweet pastry add 1 tablespoon of sugar with flour and salt.***

date scones

jam drop biscuits

biscuit pastry

Cooking time: around 15 minutes

1 egg
½ cup butter
½ cup sugar
2 cups self-raising flour

Cream butter and sugar. Add egg and mix well. Work in flour. Roll out pastry and cut out shapes. Sprinkle spices like cinnamon on the shapes. Or make a thumb impression in the centre and fill with warmed jam to make Jam Drops. Place on greased tray and bake in moderate to hot camp oven for 15 minutes until cooked.

Tip ~ Add a couple of drops of vanilla essence to the mix if you have on hand. This pastry is also ideal for a pie base, slice base and jam tarts.

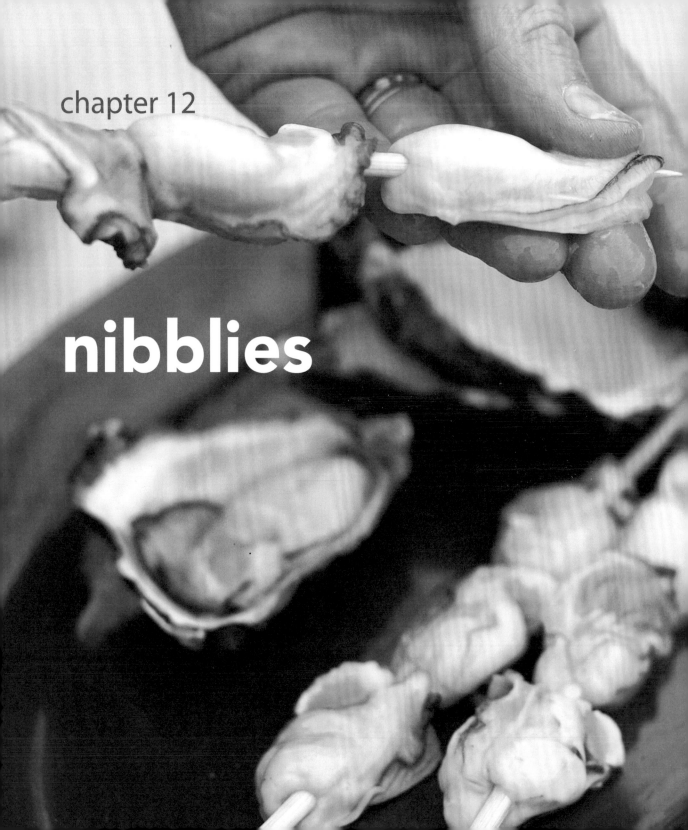

nibblies

Late afternoons relaxing beside the camp fire with a cold beverage
in hand is the perfect time to try out some of these nibblies.

cajun oysters

 Cooking time: 5-6 minutes

SERVES 2

2 tins smoked oysters or 12 large shelled oysters
1 teaspoon Cajun seasoning
¼ teaspoon dried paprika
¼ teaspoon dried basil
¼ cup plain flour
Wooden skewers
Oil or butter to fry

Combine the cajun seasoning, paprika and basil. Mix well. Reserve a teaspoon for serving. Add flour to spice mix and stir. Thread oysters onto wooden skewers. Coat with spiced flour mix. Heat oil on hot plate or in frying pan. Cook oysters until golden, about 6 minutes, turning several times. Drain on paper towel. Serve with reserved spice mix sprinkled over.

Tip ~ You can also serve these up with some mayonnaise or your choice of dipping sauce. These are a tasty way to start off a meal with an icy cold beer.

devilled nuts

Cooking time: 2-3 minutes

500 g raw nuts – peanuts, almonds, cashews etc
Oil for frying
2 teaspoons salt
2 teaspoons chilli powder

Combine salt and chilli powder. Heat oil in a frying pan. Fry the nuts one handful at a time. When golden remove and drain on absorbent paper. Once all nuts have been fried sprinkle salt and chilli mixture over nuts. When cold shake or dust off excess salt and chilli mixture and serve. Easiest way to do this is whack them in a colander and shake.

Tip ~ These nuts are easy to make whilst at camp but you could make these up before leaving home and store in an airtight container.

devilled nuts

trio of dips

nuts and bolts

300 g packet of Nutri-Grain cereal
375 g salted nuts - peanuts or cashews
1 packet cream of chicken soup
½ teaspoon dry mustard powder
½ teaspoon curry powder
½ cup oil, warmed

Mix all dry ingredients together. Pour over warmed oil and mix well. Cool and store in airtight container.

Tip ~ I love these, the only problem is they are quite moreish. This recipe makes a large quantity, but it does keep well in an airtight container, so could be made before going camping. Or do as our friend does and gives jars of nuts and bolts as a gift at Christmas.

avocado dip (craig's guacamole)

2 ripe avocados
1 small onion, finely chopped
1 medium tomato, finely chopped
¼ cup sour cream
1 tablespoon lemon juice
Tabasco to taste

Peel and seed avocados, mash flesh well with a fork. Add remaining ingredients to avocado and mix well. Serve with corn chips, on top of nachos or with bush-style mexican fajitas, see page 78

home made salsa

1 red onion, finely chopped
1 tomato, finely chopped
Juice of 1 lemon
2 teaspoons of grated lemon rind
2 tablespoons coriander chopped
½ teaspoon chilli powder

Combine all ingredients. This salsa is great served as a dip with corn chips and the avocado dip, or can be served with barbecued meat.

Tip ~ If you don't have fresh coriander replace it with 2 teaspoons of minced coriander.

ham & beer nut dip

½ packet of French Onion Soup Mix
300 ml sour cream
½ cup finely chopped ham
¼ cup chopped beer nuts

Combine all ingredients and mix well.

capsicum dip

½ packet of French Onion Soup Mix
300 ml carton sour cream
1 teaspoon of chilli powder
2 tablespoons capsicum, finely chopped

Combine all ingredients and mix well.

smoked oyster dip

125 g cream cheese
1 tin smoked oysters, drained and chopped
1 teaspoon lemon juice
Black pepper

Combine all ingredients and mix well.

*Tip ~ **For easy mixing of cream cheese, take it out
of the fridge an hour prior to using.***

sweet chilli dip

125 g cream cheese
Sweet Chilli sauce to your taste

Mix/beat cream cheese until smooth and then mix
in the sweet chilli sauce to your taste.

corn relish dip

125 g cream cheese
250 g jar of corn relish

Mix/beat cream cheese until smooth and then mix
in corn relish.

*Tip ~ **An oldie but a goodie. For easy mixing of
cream cheese, take it out of the fridge an hour
prior to using.***

smoked oyster dip

125 g cream cheese
1 tin smoked oysters, drained and chopped
1 teaspoon lemon juice
Black pepper

Combine all ingredients and mix well.

Tip ~ For easy mixing of cream cheese, take it out of the fridge an hour prior to using.

cheese straws

Cooking time: 15-20 minutes
MAKES HEAPS OF STICKS

1¼ cup plain flour
1 teaspoon salt
½ teaspoon cayenne pepper
1 cup finely grated tasty cheese
1 egg
1 egg yolk
1 tablespoon water

Combine flour, salt and cayenne pepper in a bowl. Mix in the grated cheese. Lightly beat the egg, egg yolk and water. Then pour over the flour. Mix thoroughly to a firm dough. Add extra water if necessary. Tip onto lightly floured board and roll dough out to about 5 mm thickness. Then cut strips of the dough about 5 mm wide. Place straws onto lightly greased tray and place on trivet in hot camp oven. Bake in oven with moderate coals on the base and on the lid until cooked through and golden. Cool on a rack.

Tip ~ These are great served with dip or by themselves with a drink. For a stronger flavour replace the tasty cheese with parmesan.

marinades, bastes & sauces

marinades and bastes

Marinades and bastes are great additions for helping create sumptuous meals in your bush kitchen. Why not try one next time you fire up the barbie or camp oven.

Mix all ingredients in a bowl or screw top jar unless otherwise stated, and then combine with meat and refrigerate for a couple of hours to marinate. Drain meat and reserve marinade/baste to coat meat regularly during cooking.

beef and lamb marinades

marinade 1

2 tablespoons soy sauce, ¼ cup oil, 2 teaspoons chopped onion, 1 teaspoon crushed ginger

marinade 2

¼ cup lemon juice or wine, ¼ cup oil, ½ teaspoon salt, ½ teaspoon pepper, 1 crushed garlic clove

marinade 3

¼ cup oil, 1 teaspoon Italian herbs, 1 teaspoon grated ginger, 2 crushed garlic cloves, 1 tablespoon Worcestershire sauce, ½ cup tomato sauce, ¼ cup white wine

marinade 4

½ cup red wine, 2 tablespoons oil, 2 tablespoons soy sauce, 2 crushed garlic cloves, 2 tablespoons tomato paste, 2 teaspoons Worcestershire sauce, 1 tablespoon brown sugar

marinade 5 - this one is best used for beef

¾ cup beer, 1 tablespoon honey, 2 tablespoons brown sugar, 1 teaspoon dried mustard
Method: Combine all ingredients in a saucepan and bring to the boil. Simmer for 10 minutes, then cool.

marinade 6 - this one is best used for lamb

1 tablespoon ground cumin, 1 tablespoon ground coriander, 1 teaspoon ground cinnamon, ⅓ cup plain yoghurt
Method: Combine all ingredients in a bowl with meat. Refrigerate for 3 hours.

lamb on the spit bastes

baste 1

2 cups lemon juice, 1 cup water, 1 tablespoon salt

baste 2

2 tablespoons oil, 2 tablespoons Worcestershire sauce, ½ cup vinegar, ½ cup water, ¼ cup brown sugar, ¼ cup tomato sauce, 1 tablespoon tomato paste

baste 3

¼ teaspoon hot English mustard, 2 tablespoons white wine, 2 tablespoons honey, 2 drops of Tabasco sauce, 1 teaspoon Worcestershire sauce, 1 tablespoon lemon juice, ½ cup olive oil, salt & pepper

chicken marinades

marinade 1
1 tablespoon soy sauce, ¼ cup oil, 2 teaspoons chopped onion, 1 teaspoon crushed ginger

marinade 2
3 spring onions, 2 crushed garlic cloves, 1 cup tomato sauce, 4 tablespoons beer, 1 tablespoon vinegar, 1 tablespoon honey, 1 tablespoon Tabasco sauce

marinade 3
¼ cup teriyaki sauce, ¼ cup dry sherry, 1 teaspoon crushed ginger, 1 teaspoon soft brown sugar.

marinade 4 - great with chicken or fish.
⅓ cup honey, ⅓ cup oil, 2 tablespoons Worcestershire sauce, 1 tablespoon grated orange rind, 2 crushed garlic cloves

marinade 5
½ cup soy sauce, ⅓ cup honey, 2 teaspoons ground ginger
Combine all ingredients in saucepan and heat through, brush on chicken during cooking.

marinade 6 - this can be brushed onto chicken, fish or vegetable kebabs
½ cup oil, ¼ cup white wine, 1 crushed garlic clove, ½ teaspoon dried mixed herbs, 1 teaspoon minced chilli (or one fresh chilli)

marinade 7
¼ cup lemon juice, ¼ cup oil, ½ teaspoon salt, 1 crushed garlic clove, pepper to taste, pineapple juice can be substituted for the lemon juice

marinade 8
1 tablespoon curry powder, ¼ teaspoon cinnamon, ¼ teaspoon salt, ¼ cup honey, 1 teaspoon soft butter, 2 teaspoons lemon juice, 1 teaspoon French mustard
Combine the curry powder, cinnamon and salt. Rub into chicken, let rest for 15 minutes. Barbecue or grill chicken brushing with combined honey, butter, juice and mustard.

pork marinades

marinade 1 - this is great with spare ribs
2 tablespoons olive oil, 1 crushed garlic clove, 1 teaspoon chilli powder, 1 teaspoon ginger, 2 tablespoons soy sauce, 2 tablespoons English mustard, 2 tablespoons lemon juice

marinade 2 - this can be used with pork or beef
1 cup pineapple juice, 2 tablespoons honey, 1 tablespoon soy sauce, 2 teaspoons crushed ginger.
Combine all ingredients and brush on meat during cooking.

marinade 3 - another great marinade for spare ribs
3 tablespoons soy sauce, 1 tablespoon honey, 1 tablespoon brown vinegar, 1 teaspoon curry powder, 3 tablespoons tomato sauce, 1 tablespoon sherry, 2 crushed garlic cloves, 1 tablespoon crushed ginger, 2 tablespoons sweet chilli sauce

marinade 4 - this is can be brushed over pork, beef or even sausages
4 tablespoons red wine, ½ cup honey, ¼ teaspoon ground chilli, 1 teaspoon mustard powder

glazing pork chops

creamy bacon & mushroom sauce

 Cooking time: around 20 minutes

SERVES 4

4 rashers of bacon, chopped
1 onion, chopped
2 cups of mushrooms, sliced
Crushed garlic to taste
300 ml carton cream
1 tablespoon grated parmesan cheese
Good dash Worcestershire sauce
Black pepper

Fry bacon, onion and garlic in a little oil until tender Add mushrooms and heat through. Place pan over moderate coals and add cream, parmesan cheese, Worcestershire sauce and pepper to taste. Cook over low heat stirring until sauce thickens – do not let boil. Serve over pasta of choice.

Tip ~ Evaporated milk can replace the cream for a lighter sauce.

spicy tomato & bacon sauce for pasta

Cooking time: around 20 minutes

SERVES 4

6 bacon rashers, rind removed and diced
1 onion, chopped
1 garlic clove, crushed
420 g tinned crushed tomatoes
140 g tin tomato paste
Chilli powder to taste
Tabasco sauce
Italian herbs
1 tablespoon sliced black olives, optional

Fry bacon, onion and garlic in hot oil in frying pan. Add crushed tomatoes, tomato paste, chilli powder, Tabasco sauce to taste, a good sprinkle of Italian herbs and olives if using. Move to lower heat and simmer for 15 minutes until sauce thickens. Serve over pasta of choice with parmesan cheese.

christmas
in the bush

Glazed ham and roast turkey with all the trimmings and Christmas pudding from your bush kitchen—no worries with these hassle-free recipes for Christmas lunch and dinner in the bush. Included in this section are a few different recipe ideas for your Christmas lunch or dinner. Instead of carrying a leg of ham or a turkey, which take up quite a bit of room, try the glazed tinned ham or the glazed turkey breasts. And in case there is a total fire ban on Christmas Day, we've included a range of special festive salads that are tasty and filling, as well as easy to prepare. And for afters, there is the no fuss Christmas pudding.

glazed ham

Carrying a leg of ham is obviously going to take up some valuable storage space in your car fridge or esky. However, you can still have a glazed ham on Christmas day in the bush. This glazed tinned ham not only takes up little room, but it still looks and tastes great.

 Cooking time: around 30-45 minutes
SERVES 3-4

450 g can leg or shoulder ham
Whole cloves
Glaze of choice – see below

Arrange cloves decoratively on top and sides of ham. Place ham in tray or dish. Combine glaze ingredients and brush over ham. Bake in camp oven with coals on bottom and lid for around 30-45 minutes. Baste with glaze a couple of times during cooking. Bake until glaze is golden and ham is heated through.

mustard glaze

2 tablespoons seeded mustard, 2 tablespoons honey, ¼ cup orange juice

Mix all ingredients

apricot glaze

⅔ cup apricot nectar, ¼ cup brown sugar, 2 tablespoons honey, 1 tablespoon Dijon mustard

Mix all ingredients in a small saucepan and stir over low heat until sugar and honey is dissolved and well mixed

ginger glaze

⅓ cup honey, ¼ cup chopped glace ginger, ¼ cup brown sugar, 1½ tablespoons water

Mix all ingredients in a small saucepan and stir over low heat until sugar and honey is dissolved and well mixed.

roast turkey

The easiest type of turkey to carry is one of the ready to roast rolled turkey breasts or thighs which can be purchased from the supermarket. Remember that these will need to be defrosted for 24-48 hours prior to cooking. Also consider ready-to-cook turkey breast or thigh – the size will depend on the number of people to feed.

  Cooking time: around 1½-2 hours
SERVES 4-6

1 x rolled turkey breast

Place the turkey onto a trivet in a hot camp oven, then cook the turkey for 1½ to 2 hours, until cooked, with hot coals on the lid of the camp oven and around the base. Check regularly to ensure meat is cooking evenly and brush glaze over turkey.

glazed turkey breasts

Cooking time: around 10-15 minutes
SERVES 4

4 turkey breast fillets
Glaze of choice – see below

Cook turkey breast fillets on lightly oiled barbecue plate or in oiled frying pan, 4-6 minutes each side, brushing with glaze whilst cooking.

orange glaze

2 tablespoons orange marmalade, 1 tablespoon orange juice, 1 tablespoon mustard powder, 1 tablespoon brown sugar

Combine all ingredients and mix well.

apple glaze

¼ cup apple juice, ⅓ cup melted butter, ⅓ cup honey

Combine all ingredients and mix well.

last minute christmas pudding

last minute christmas pudding

Forgotten all about a Christmas pudding? Here's a simple solution which tastes great.

 Cooking time: 15 minutes
SERVES 6-8

1 store bought fruit cake
¾ cup of your choice of either rum, brandy, sherry or apple juice
Foil and greaseproof paper

Take cake out of packaging and place on a baking tray. Prick cake all over with a skewer. Cover cake with some foil and heat in a camp oven for about 15 minutes. Remove from oven and pour ½ cup of chosen liquid over hot cake. When liquid has been absorbed, pour over balance of liquid. Wait for cake to cool and for all liquid to be absorbed. Wrap cake in greaseproof paper then foil until ready to serve.

Tip ~ The longer the cake is left the better the flavour.

bush style christmas pudding

Cooking time: 2-2½ hours
SERVES 6-8

2 cups mixed dried fruit
½ cup butter
¾ cup white sugar
2 teaspoons bicarbonate of soda
1 cup cold strong black tea
1 teaspoon mixed spice
4 cups plain flour
Pinch salt

Cream the butter and white sugar. This will take a while doing it by hand, but be persistent. Dissolve the bicarbonate of soda in the cold tea. Add to tea the creamed butter and sugar, the mixed spice, flour, salt and fruit. Mix well. Pour mixture into a greased 8 cup pudding basin or dish. Cover with two layers of greaseproof paper and tie. Let stand overnight. Place pudding basin or dish into camp oven and add enough water to go half way up side of dish. Steam for 2-2½ hours. Serve with hot custard.

meals for a no cook christmas

As Christmas is in the height of our fire danger season there are times that a total fire ban may be imposed on Christmas Day. Don't despair; we've included some no cook special salads to have on these days. The seafood salads are great for those camping near the coast.

salami & bean salad

SERVES **4**

125 g salami, thinly sliced and cut into stripas
1 can red kidney beans, drained and rinsed
1 can butter beans, drained and rinsed
125 g mushrooms, sliced
6 black olives, pitted and sliced
4 shallots, chopped
1 punnet cherry tomatoes, halved

DRESSING
¼ cup olive oil
2 tablespoons red wine vinegar
1 garlic clove, crushed

Combine salami, beans, mushrooms, olives and shallots in a bowl. Combine all dressing ingredients in a screw top jar and shake well. Add tomatoes just prior to serving and pour dressing over salad.

prawn salad

SERVES **4**

1 kg cooked medium/king prawns
1 large can of corn kernels, drained
1 punnet cherry tomatoes, halved
1 capsicum, chopped
1 avocado, sliced
1 lettuce

DRESSING
1 cup mayonnaise
2 tablespoons lemon juice
1 garlic clove, crushed
Few drops of Tabasco sauce

Peel prawns and combine with corn, tomatoes, capsicum, avocado and torn lettuce in bowl. Combine all dressing ingredients and pour over salad.

prawn & salmon salad

SERVES **4**

500 g cooked prawns shelled and deveined,
tails intact
440 g can pineapple pieces, drained; reserve juice
220 g can red salmon, drained
1 capsicum , sliced
Lettuce

DRESSING
¼ cup mayonnaise
2 tablespoons juice from pineapple
1 tablespoon cream
1 tablespoon tomato sauce

Break salmon into pieces, skin and bones removed. Combine salmon, prawns, pineapple and capsicum in bowl. Place lettuce on plates and serve prawn mixture on lettuce. Combine all dressing ingredients and pour dressing over salad.

fish salad

SERVES **6**

2 x 485 g tin of red salmon or tuna
¼ cup lemon juice
4 cucumbers, sliced
1 punnet cherry tomatoes, halved
Lettuce
3 radishes, sliced (optional)

DRESSING
⅓ cup oil
2 tablespoon lemon juice
1 clove garlic crushed

Place well drained fish in bowl with lemon juice, cucumbers, tomatoes and radishes and mix in dressing. Place lettuce on serving plate and top with fish mixture. Combine all dressing ingredients in a jar and shake well. Pour dressing over salad.

Tip ~ Be sure to remove skin and bones if using salmon.

chicken & apple salad

SERVES **4**

1 barbecue chicken
½ red cabbage, shredded
3 apples, cored and sliced
½ cup chopped walnuts

DRESSING
1½ cups natural yoghurt
2 teaspoons lemon juice
2 teaspoons of mustard
Salt and pepper to taste

Take all meat off chicken, and cut into small pieces. Combine chicken, cabbage, apples and walnuts in bowl. Combine all dressing ingredients in a small bowl and mix well. Pour over dressing and mix to coat well.

*Tip ~ **Use your favourite mustard in the dressing.***

devils marbles

fast food

In need of a feed in a hurry? Then here are a few
ideas for quick and simple meals while on the go.
Although holidays are about taking it easy, relaxing and
enjoying yourself, there are occasions when you'll be
pressed for time — this is when you can use a few of the
following ideas to cobble together an enjoyable meal
in a matter of minutes.

hot dogs

Purchase your hot dogs in cryoyvac packs or in tins. Pull out the gas stove and boil up the hot dogs and place them in some fresh bread, add some grated cheese, sauce and mustard. You can even quickly fry up an onion.

jaffles

If you're out in the bush, it doesn't take too long to make a small fire to get some hot coals for a toasted jaffle sandwich - or you can even use your gas burner. Jaffles always seem to taste best with cheese in them. For savoury fillings try ham, cheese, tomato, onion, tuna, bacon, mushrooms, salami, olives, capsicum, leftovers from the night before, pineapple, egg, baked beans, tinned spaghetti, chicken, tinned stews. For sweet fillings try apples sprinkled with sugar, peaches with ground cloves, banana, pineapple. You can also use fruit bread instead of plain bread for a change.

pan fried sandwiches

If you don't have a jaffle iron or not enough time to make a fire, then pull out the gas stove, a frying pan and an egg flip. Make up your sandwiches, butter the outside of the bread and fry in hot pan on both sides until golden. Good fillings include ham, cheese, tomato, onion, salami.

wraps

Lavish bread, flour tortillas and pitas are great alternatives to bread, and generally keep longer. Fill with your favourite filling, roll up and enjoy. If you're at camp and have coals, you can also fill these up, wrap them in foil and heat in the camp oven.

sausage or steak sandwiches

From time to time when we're passing through a town around lunch time, we make use of the local park, especially if it has electric or gas BBQs. We'll often grab some fresh bread or rolls, a couple of snags or even a spicy kransky from the local butcher or deli and cook them up with some onion for sausage sangers. Alternatively grab a nice piece of steak and cook that up on the barbeque with some salad and nice fresh bread for a great steak sandwich. Nice and easy and there's no washing up! Otherwise if not in town, stoke up the fire and BBQ on a hot grill plate or pull out the frying pan and fry up over your gas cooker.

brewing the perfect cuppa

The time-honoured art of making billy tea!

the time-honoured art of making billy tea!

One point to cause a bone of contention around a camp fire must surely be the 'correct' method involved in making the perfect cup of billy tea. It seems no two people can wholeheartedly agree on the best recipe for the bushman's brew.

This aside, the following method does always seem to produce the desired results. Give it a try and see if you too will be converted to billy tea.

Firstly, you need to get the water to a good rolling boil in the billy. Make sure that you use good, clean fresh water. If you are using a new billy for the first time make sure that you get the outside nice and black first. Never clean the outside of your billy. Folklore suggests that a green twig placed across the top of the billy while it is on the fire helps reduce the smokey flavour of billy tea. However, I am not convinced of its merit.

Once the water is at a rolling boil and the billy is still on the fire toss your measured amount of tea leaves into the billy. Generally, this would be the amount that would fit in the cup of the palm of your hand or one teaspoon for each person and one for the billy. Some people add a couple of green gum leaves at this point. Try it and see what you think.

Now, the timing is important. You need to let the tea leaves stew for a brief time before removing the billy from the fire. Most reckon about 30 to 45 seconds to be adequate. What happens here is that the tannins from the tea are released by the short boiling process, giving your cuppa its unique taste and colour. If the tea leaves are boiled for too long the resulting cuppa will have a marked bitter taste. Remove the billy from the fire and place on the ground.

The next trick is to settle the tea leaves to the bottom of the billy. The best method is by tapping the side of the billy about half a dozen times with a stick. It's not a good idea to 'swing' the billy in a large arc over your shoulder to help settle the tea leaves. People have ended up with serious scalds from this practice.

Let the billy stand for a minute or two to allow the brew to 'draw', then carefully pour your bush brew into mugs. Purists suggest that billy tea should be drunk straight—that is without sugar or milk. But I'll have mine white, thanks. Enjoy!

australian terms

Don't know the difference between a Teamster and a Trapper or a Ringer and a Rouseabout? A number of old Australian terms have been used throughout this book, here's the lowdown on their meanings and a few others as well.

Backblocks — A term that is used to denote a rural area other than the remote, unsettled outback regions.

Baitlayer — Often in drovers camps as a joke, drovers would refer to the cook as a 'baitlayer', or in other words his cooking was that bad he was a poisoner.

Beardies — A general term used to describe two bearded bushmen from the New England region in northern New South Wales during the 1830s. Subsequently, new squatters to the area were also known as 'Beardies'. The area bounded by Inverell and Glen Innes is still known today as 'the land of the Beardies'.

The Black Stump — A mythical landmark that is the border between the settled areas and the remote uninhabited regions. The 'original' black stump is claimed to lie just to the north of the central western New South Wales town of Coolah.

Bluey - Roll of blankets – swag.

Burdekin Duck — According to Bill Harney's Cook Book, Burdekin Duck is a bushman's dish made with cold corned beef. Slices of beef were dipped in a batter of flour, baking powder and milk with finely chopped onions and fried in hot dripping until brown.

Bush Trifle — Layered Johnny Cakes spread with jam, with condensed milk poured over.

Bushman's Clock — The laughing kookaburra is commonly known as the Bushmans Clock.

Bushman's Hot Dinner — Bill Fern-Wannan in his book Australian Folklore describes a bushman's hot dinner as a meal of damper and mustard.

Cobbler — A shearer's term referring to the last sheep left in the pen at the end of a days shearing.

Cocky's Joy — Golden Syrup or Treacle.

Colonial Goose — Boned leg of mutton seasoned with stuffing made of sage and onion.

Cooee — A far reaching call used in the bush to attract attention.

Damper — A bush bread made from flour and water and baked in the ashes of a camp fire or in a camp oven.

Diamantina Cocktail — A drink originating in Queensland consisting of Bundaberg Rum, condensed milk and an emu's egg.

Digger — The name given to gold miners on the early goldfields. Later used to refer to Australian soldiers from the First World War onward.

Dinkum — To be dinkum, or fair dinkum is to be honest, reliable and genuine. The term is said to have arisen from the mispronunciation by a Chinese grog shanty owner of 'fair drinking' in the 1850s.

Donga — Hut or shelter; also a gully or channel formed by the action of water.

Doughboy — A boiled flour dumpling.

Drover — A stockman who drives cattle or sheep to market over a long distance, usually in the outback. They commonly used stock routes such as the famous Birdsville Track.

birdsville hotel, outback queensland

Dungaree Settler — An early Australian small farmer during colonial times who was too poor to wear any other type of clothing except for the faded blue cotton clothes made in India.

Duckshove — To be unscrupulous in dealings; avoiding responsibility.

Duff — Currant pudding.

Emu-bobber — A person who is employed to clean up an area by hand.

Fat Cake — A damper fried in fat.

Flour Bag — A term for someone who's hair or beard is going white.

Fossicker's Dinner — Consisting of bread, dripping and a roast onion.

Furphy — A rumour or tall story. This term originated in the First World War when the drivers of the Furphy water carts brought rumours to the troops.

Grabben Gullen Pie — According to Bill Harney's Cook Book, a Grabben Gullen Pie, or Possum Pumpkin Pie was made from a possum that was cleaned and cut up then roasted in a hollowed out pumpkin until the meat was cooked.

Hargraves — Edward Hammond Hargraves laid claim as the discoverer of gold in Australia at Ophir, New South Wales in 1851. A central west New South Wales village also bears his name.

Hawker — A travelling salesman who often used a horse and wagon to sell his wares which would include everything from pots and pans to lotions and potions.

Hump — To carry a swag, eg: hump a bluey.

Jackaroo — The name given to a young man working on a cattle or sheep grazing property to gain experience before becoming an overseer, station manager or moving onto his own place.

Jumbuck — Young lamb.

Long Paddock — The name for stock routes.

Mud Pirate — One of a number of terms given to the river boatmen of the Murray-Darling Rivers during the days of paddle-steamers. Others include inside sailor and freshwater seamen.

Murrumbidgee Jam — A slice of bread dipped in cold tea and sprinkled with sugar—preferably brown sugar.

Never Never — Refers to the far outback.

New Chum — Nineteenth century newly arrived immigrants, mostly from Britain. New chums were often the butt of practical jokes by old hands.

Overland Trout — A goanna, or any large lizard cooked in the ashes of an open fire were often called overland trout.

Paroo Sandwich — A 'meal' consisting of beer and wine mixed together is known as a Paroo Sandwich.

Quart-pot — A billy that holds a quart of water.

Ringer — Either a stockman or a champion shearer—usually the 'gun' shearer who shears the highest tally of sheep in the shed over a given period.

Rouseabout — Someone employed on stations to do odd jobs. In the shearing shed the 'Rousey' gathers up the clip and sweeps the floor among other jobs.

Shiralee — A type of swag or bedroll and shaped like a leg of mutton. It was carried slung over the shoulder by a strap or piece of rope and was usually balanced by a tucker bag resting on the chest.

Silver City — A name often used for Broken Hill due to its productive lead-zinc mines.

Smoko — Term for tea break and also used for the food and drink supplied at this time.

Spotted Dog — A boiled pudding. Also known as Spotted Dick.

Stockman — Someone who works on a grazing property to handle cattle or sheep.

Stockman's Dinner — A cigarette and a spit make up a Stockman's Dinner.

Sundowner — A swagman who arrived at a property or station late in the afternoon around nightfall when it was too late to work, but still obtained food and shelter for the night. Sundowners usually left early the next morning!

Swaggie — A man who travelled on foot carrying a swag or bedroll. He survived by doing odd jobs or from handouts. Swaggies were commonplace during the early days of settlement and during the depression years.

Teamster — Another term for Bullockie.

Tuck-out — A meal.

Tucker-bag — A bag which bushmen and swaggies carried their food (tucker) in.

Underground Mutton — A term used for rabbits.

Whaler — Bush nomad; someone who can exist without working.

boiling billy

Guides for Aussie bush travellers

If you're going bush, however you're going bush, there's a guide from Boiling Billy you'll want to take along. These new guides are illustrated with full-colour photography and packed with helpful hints and tried-and-tested tips.

9781922131003 • Australian Camp Oven Cooking • $34.99

9781921683923 • Classic Outback Tracks • $39.95

9781921874789 • Robert Pepper's 4WD Handbook • $44.95

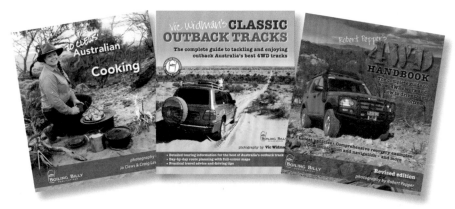

Boiling Billy's Camping Guide to Australia

Boiling Billy's Camping Guide to Australia is the complete guide to over 3,000 camping areas all across the country with campsites beside the beach through to the mountains and the vast outback. Along with the huge array of sites, this comprehensive new guide features an Australia-wide touring atlas showing the location of each and every campsite, detailed information on the facilities and activities on offer along with concise access information and recommendations for the author's own favourite spots, all gleaned from more than 17 years of travelling Australia. Boiling Billy is Australia's premier camping series, and you can be sure each of their bestselling books provide honest, reliable information.

9781922131119 • $49.99

If your local bookshop does not have stock of a Boiling Billy or Woodslane book, they can easily order it for you. In case of difficulty please contact our customer service team on 02 8445 2300 or info@woodslane.com.au.

recipe index